Let
the
Light
In

Also by Jane McDonald:

Riding the Waves
Follow Your Dreams

Let the Light In

Lessons learned through love, life and laughter

Jane McDonald

EBURY
SPOTLIGHT

Ebury Spotlight, an imprint of Ebury Publishing
One Embassy Gardens
8 Viaduct Gardens
Nine Elms
London SW11 7BW

Ebury Spotlight is part of the Penguin Random House
group of companies whose addresses can be found
at global.penguinrandomhouse.com

First published by Ebury Spotlight in 2024

www.penguin.co.uk

A CIP catalogue record for this book is available from the British Library

ISBN 9781529936919

Printed and bound in Great Britain by Clays Ltd, Elcograf S.p.A.

The authorised representative in the EEA is Penguin Random House Ireland,
Morrison Chambers, 32 Nassau Street, Dublin D02 YH68

Penguin Random House is committed to a sustainable future for
our business, our readers and our planet. This book is made
from Forest Stewardship Council® certified paper.

'I want to do a knee
slide into death with
a bottle of champagne
in my hand, saying
"What a life that
was!"'

CONTENTS

PROLOGUE

We're all on a learning curve, our whole life long. Some take the slow and steady road, carefully stepping over potholes and avoiding hairpin bends. Others strap themselves in for a big dipper ride through dizzy highs and crashing lows. And then there are the trapeze artists, learning to fly while walking on wire. No matter how many times they fall and hit the ground, how hard the wind is blowing or who knocks them off course, they always get back on.

What's it been like for me? I think writing this book is going to give me more answers than I have right now, but my current thinking is 'flying the trapeze, in a hurricane, on board a ship'! What's kept me going is the sunshine on the horizon, because no matter how tough things get, the sun does always rise again. And every time I see the morning sun, it's through clearer eyes, because the day before has taught me something new.

I've experienced more rejection than acceptance. This builds up resilience and makes you improve, so don't give up.

I've had more doors slammed in my face than opened. If there's a wall in front of you then find a way to either go over it, under it or around it. Don't just walk away.

I've experienced more heartbreak than love in my relationships. Rejection in your personal life is okay, as it makes you appreciate love when it arrives.

I've lost touch with more friends than I've kept. I truly believe we meet people for a reason and I also believe they leave us when the time is right. Some stay the course and some don't, and that's okay too.

I have earned more money than I've ever had to show for it. Being hungry for your passion makes you work even harder.

I have failed more times than I've won. You must fail to be a success, you must lose to win. That's called learning the craft.

FOREWORD

Five years ago, when I wrote my autobiography, I didn't imagine I'd be putting pen to paper again. After 20 years in show business and surviving some very stormy waters, I was on the crest of a wave, cruising the world making my own BAFTA-winning TV series and looking forward to a sold-out tour with the best band I'd ever worked with. To complete the dream, I had my lovely partner, Ed, waiting for me back home in Wakefield.

The next chapters of my life were already glistening on the horizon, but nobody would read about those. Me and Ed were going to spend more time together (to be fair, I had been on 45 cruises!) and after the tour ended in 2020 I was looking forward to drifting into retirement. 'Leave the party while you're still having fun' is one of my mottos in life, and that's exactly what I was planning to do, so that me and Ed could enjoy our golden years at our own, leisurely pace.

Tragically, fate had other plans, and instead of sailing into the sunset with the love of my life, I had to say farewell to Ed in March 2021. His untimely passing broke me, completely.

The title of this book is borrowed from one of my songs, and 'Let the Light In' means a great deal to me for lots of reasons. First of all I'm very proud it's become one of my biggest hits with fans in recent years. They say the song lifts their spirits and inspires them, whether they've had a bad day at the office or are dealing with something far worse. That is music to my ears, because to me there is no greater reward than cheering someone up, putting a smile on their face and spreading joy and positivity. It's what I go to work for.

A lot of people thought I wrote 'Let the Light In' during tough times in lockdown, or as a way of coping with losing Ed, but in fact I wrote it more than 20 years ago, at another very low point in my life. I'd expected 15 minutes of fame after appearing in the BBC docusoap *The Cruise* in 1998, but instead I was catapulted to instant stardom. Nobody was more surprised than me. My debut album shot to number one and over the next four years I was caught in a showbiz whirlwind, hosting my own primetime TV shows and performing in theatres of my dreams, including the Blackpool Opera House, London Palladium and MGM Grand in Las Vegas. When it all went wrong in 2002 I lost *everything* – my marriage, my career, my glamorous life in Florida and every penny I had ever earned. I moved back in with my mother in Wakefield, hiding away in my bedroom, smarting with pain and humiliation and feeling terrified of what the future held.

I don't remember how or exactly when, but somewhere in that very dark period in my life 'Let the Light In' was taking shape inside my head, as songs have a habit of doing. When I eventually sat down at my old piano again, something went 'whoosh' and all the lyrics came tumbling out. 'Life is what you make it,' I sang. 'Happy endings are for making . . . It's up to you to take one step and make a start.'

I don't believe we are meant to live in misery or sadness; finding joy is our purpose in life. Whatever I've been through and however many doors have been slammed in my face, that belief has always been there, deep inside. 'Let the Light In' was a reminder to myself that my life was in my hands, and it was up to me to climb out of the doldrums and into the light. After Ed died, I had to find the strength to do it all over again. It was the hardest thing I've ever had to do, but that song helped me get back to where I am today, embracing life and looking forward to my next adventures, whatever they may be.

* * *

When I sang 'Let the Light In' on my 2022 tour it was absolutely fantastic to look out into the audience and see smiling faces as my fans sang the words back to me: *Look inside your heart and tell me what you see. Close your eyes and dream of who you want to be . . . Stand up and be counted, be who you want to be.*

One night after a show, I turned to my best friend, Sue Ravey, and said, 'You know what? It's been like my career, has that song.'

'What are you on about now?' Sue said, as she often does when I babble on.

'What I mean is, it's been through hell and high water to get to where it is today!'

We both laughed like drains.

'Well, if we didn't laugh we'd cry,' Sue said dryly.

* * *

I vividly remember the first time I played 'Let the Light In' to a musical director, probably sometime in the mid-2000s.

'I want to record this song,' I said. 'I think it will go down well.'

'No, Jane,' he said firmly, shaking his head. 'It's not your best. Let's look at something else.'

I was frustrated and disheartened, but there was nothing I could do. For years I tried again and again with the next musical director and the next, suggesting it for album after album and show after show.

'No,' each one said, shaking his head and refusing to budge.

'I know I'm not the best songwriter,' I said. 'I've never claimed to be. I'm not even the best singer. But I feel so strongly that I know my fans, and I'm telling you they will *love* this song, because it comes from the heart and it will lift them up.'

'It's still a no, Jane. Sorry. It really isn't good enough I'm afraid. We're doing this cover instead . . .'

I got more riled every time. I knew in my gut that 'Let the Light In' was not just good enough to record, but had the potential to be a fan favourite. Still, for the best part of 15 years I stupidly handed my power to all these men, letting them have the final say and telling me 'no, you can't do it'.

It's just as well I'm not a quitter. In 2018, when Seán Barry came on board as my new musical director (MD) and a new tour and album were in the offing, I still hadn't let it drop.

'Please give this a listen,' I said.

As always, I couldn't help having a smile of my face as I sang the song, because the lyrics make me feel so positive and joyful.

Let the light in, make a difference, be somebody . . . Nothing in this world is gonna stop you now. Baby, take my hand and I will show you how.

When I looked up from the piano I saw that Seán was smiling too.

'Mmm.' He nodded thoughtfully. 'It could be great, Jane. We just need to slow it down and that will give it a really good gospel feel.'

'Really?' I thought. 'Did he really just say that?'

It was a fabulous moment. Seán got me! He is a man with incredible talent and such great vision, and he got me! I could hardly believe it. Seán was treating me like an artist and not just 'that girl off *The Cruise* who'd done well but really shouldn't still be here'. I can't tell you how happy and grateful I felt, because that's what it had been like throughout my career, it really had.

* * *

'Let the Light In' is a song that will always remind me of how much I've learned, how far I have come and, most of all, how good things happen when you open up your heart and keep holding on to your dreams. You've *got* to get yourself out of the darkness when you find yourself there. I have been in the deepest depths, but every time I refused to go under, as hard as it was to keep myself going. After losing Ed it seemed impossible, but here I am, back living my best life, just as he would have wanted me to.

From everything I have experienced, including all the mistakes I've made over the years, I've always moved forward knowing something more about life and how to make the most of it, come what may. If sharing all the lessons I've learned on my journey can help other people to keep chasing their dreams, conquer their fears and find more joy in life, I'll be so chuffed.

I hope you enjoy reading my book.

CHAPTER ONE

CONQUERING ANXIETY

'There's always a solution'

'What's gone on?' I thought, feeling my phone buzzing in my pocket.

I was at the wedding of two members of my band in Croatia in June 2023, enjoying my first proper holiday in eight years.

The phone buzzed again. And again.

My family and friends knew I was at the wedding, most of the band and Sue were out there too, and work knew not to contact me. Who could it be?

When I felt the phone vibrate yet again I started to think somebody must have died, and as soon as the ceremony was over I slipped away to look at my phone. There were umpteen missed calls, all from the same number – my agent. I called him straight away.

'This better be good,' I said.

'It's the *Soap Awards*,' he replied. 'They want you to present them, on Saturday.'

'Flipping hell! The *Soap Awards*! Yes, please. Get me on a plane!'

It was already Wednesday. I'd need to fly home the next day, do the rehearsal on Friday and present the show on the Saturday night. 'That's how I like a job!' I thought. The wedding celebrations would be over by then, and so I'd only be missing out on a few days on a sun lounger. Then I could fly back to Croatia to finish my holiday on the Sunday.

'You're a national treasure, Jane!' a couple of close friends said when they found out what I was up to.

'Give over,' I replied, pointing out that ITV had to find a replacement for Phillip Schofield at the last minute. 'They're desperate,' I joked, 'that's all this is!' But really and truly, who was I trying to kid? Last-minute replacement or not, this was a huge honour, and I was over the moon to be asked to step in.

I've been a lifelong soap fan, but this was about much more than presenting awards to so many actors I admire. It's been a fight all the way up with me and my career, both in music and TV, but that was all firmly in the past. Now I had people at the top who championed me and rated me, and I can't tell you how validating that feels.

The *Soap Awards* were being held at the Lowry theatre in Salford Quays, one of my all-time favourite venues and a place that always feels like home when I perform there on tour. Usually the first four rows are packed with faces so familiar to me it's like performing to members of my family. 'Why don't you go to Barbados instead of following me around?' I tease. The fans know I don't mean a word of it. I love them to bits, my shows would not be the same without them, and every time I see them I feel so grateful for their loyalty.

Despite always feeling so well supported on stage, by my band as well as the audience, I still get nervous before I go on, my throat drying up and perspiration prickling the palms of my hands. Backstage, me and the band have a little ritual, all getting in a circle, putting our hands in and going 'wooooooooooh', before throwing our arms up in the air, giving a high five or a cheer and saying 'have a good one'. It helps settle my nerves, because it's a reminder we're all in this together, and we have each other's back.

I used to have a drink before a show, knocking back a Drambuie or a brandy in an attempt to stop the nerves snapping like knicker elastic all around my body. But those days are gone. Seán, my MD, has banned alcohol before a show. We can do what we like afterwards, and I do like a glass of wine from time to time, but the rule now is not one sip beforehand. I totally support this. Not only is it the professional thing to do but the alcohol didn't even work, because whatever you do there will *always* be nerves before a show. And that's precisely how it should be.

'Nerves are the respect I show my audience,' I've said many times, because if I just bowled up without a tremor, what would that say? The day that happened I'd have to pack it in, because it would mean I didn't care.

Over the years I've learned to embrace the nerves as a vital part of the build-up and the show. It means my adrenaline is pumping and I'm gearing up to give my all on stage. When you're putting on a show you have to have the right energy, or what my mother used to call 'good vibrations', in order to connect with the audience and put on the best possible performance. And making sure everybody has a fantastic night is what it's all about.

* * *

Backstage at the Lowry, dolled up in a glittering gold gown, my nerves were biting just enough to set me up for the show, but I wasn't feeling anxious. In fact I was surprised at how calm I was. I'm used to performing live, and I told myself I had nothing to be worried about. Presenting the *Soap Awards* involves a lot of reading Autocue. I'd do a bit of ad libbing of course – I can't help myself – but really this would be a walk in the park compared to putting on my own show, performing beneath a 30-foot-high sign on stage that says JANE in a blaze of silver lights.

If my inner dialogue makes me sound overly confident, I make no apology. I don't like cockiness or arrogance; nobody else needs to hear the conversations we have inside our heads to gear ourselves up. But it's so important to believe in yourself, because when your doubts and worries are under control your self-esteem rises, and that's when the magic happens.

'If I were a bar of chocolate I'd eat mysen' is a phrase I've thought to myself many times, and I deliberately use the Yorkshire word for myself, because I'm so proud of who I am and where I come from. When I say it out loud, as I have on occasion, it always makes people laugh. But it's not a joke. We *all* need to love ourselves. So many people in the music and TV industries have tried to change me over the years, and it's been an uphill battle just to stay being me, but I persevered and I've done it. It *had* to be done, because if you're not allowed to be yourself, what chance have you got of loving the person you are, and living your best life?

* * *

Looking out from the wings at the sea of famous faces packed into the Lowry, I took a deep breath and had a little moment to myself, drinking it all in.

Chapter One

Who'd have thought I'd ever be here, doing this?

Images of myself as a sickly, skinny little girl, trembling with nerves, flickered across my mind. If you knew me as a child you would never have believed I'd make my living performing on any stage, let alone this one tonight, surrounded by the gods of British television and some of the biggest names in TV drama. As for presenting my own TV shows over the years, being a Loose Woman, travelling the world making holiday shows and playing to packed arenas, who would have wagered on that?

I was a child who 'lived on her nerves'; that's the way people described me when I was growing up. I've never really understood why I was like that, although looking back on my childhood, and writing about it here, has helped me shine new light on it.

Despite the fact that my mother was a fabulous cook, I always struggled to eat the food on my plate. I was painfully thin, constantly sick and I'd jump out of my skin whenever I heard loud noises, or even when the telephone rang. I also suffered terribly with travel sickness. My brother, Tony, couldn't believe it when I vomited over the handlebars of my new bike the first time he took me out on it. Dad had found the bicycle frame dumped at the back of our house and he sprayed it gold, added wheels and gave it to me for Christmas. I was so thrilled, but I barely went round the corner before I started throwing up. 'I just don't believe this,' Tony said, slapping his forehead. 'Nobody gets bicycle sick.' Well, I did, and my delicate stomach was so debilitating I much preferred staying indoors to going out anywhere, because at least I could be sick in our toilet if I needed to be.

Nobody could explain where this anxious, queasy little girl had come from. My parents had moved from their native Scotland to Yorkshire for work in the mid 1950s, along with my sister Janet, a baby then, and several other members of the family, including my mum's mum. By the time I arrived on 4 April 1963, Janet was nine, my brother Tony was five and our family home was a big Victorian house in Eastmoor Road, on the posh side of Wakefield. The coal fire was always lit and the smell of fresh laundry and home-cooked food filled the air. It felt like a safe haven, and it was the place I loved to be more than anywhere in the world. As the baby of the family, I was doted on, and I was in no doubt I was loved and cherished by both my parents.

Dad was a miner, working at the coalface so as to earn the best possible wage in the pit, but even so our large home doubled as a boarding house to help pay the bills. Mum had pushed for this step up the property ladder. She was always aspirational, was my mother, while Dad would have much preferred to stay in the smaller house they had before, pay off the mortgage and have a quieter, simpler life.

Gran moved in with us and helped Mum look after the constant stream of lodgers who came and went, and in my earliest memories I'm sitting alone in the parlour, listening to music on the radio and waving from the window to people waiting at the bus stop below. I was no more than a toddler, but I remember being perfectly happy on my own while Mum and Gran washed the linen, changed the beds and prepared every meal from scratch. Whenever they checked on me they were always amazed at how quiet and contented I was.

'She's such an intelligent bairn,' Mum said proudly the first time they saw me waving to the people outside. 'Aye,' said Gran, 'there's something a wee bit special about that one, and it could well be she's preparing for her destiny.'

My Gran was a member of the Wakefield Spiritualist Church and had a gift for clairvoyance, and by God, you really did need psychic abilities to predict my future back then! I was never one of those kids who got up on the coffee table at Christmas and sang to the family. I didn't have that in me at all; my nervous stomach would have done somersaults just thinking about performing to an audience of any kind.

Despite whatever it was that Gran picked up on, all the early evidence suggested that my destiny was to have a very quiet life indeed, doing something that didn't push me out of my comfort zone, require me to travel or eat anything but the plainest of foods. I was sick on the coach every time I went on a school trip, sick at the fairground, sick on the bus and sick just looking at the food on my dinner plate. My parents couldn't even tell me when we were going on holiday to the caravan park in Bridlington, because I'd immediately feel nauseous just thinking about the drive there in Dad's clapped-out old van.

When my brother and sister got up to mischief, it made my guts twist with worry. I desperately wanted to shout 'stop it!' but I was too timid and anxious to do anything but keep my mouth shut. One time, very unusually, I joined in a water fight with squeezy bottles and ruined the brand new wallpaper in our extremely tall hallway and landing. Even though I was the one who caused the damage, Janet and Tony took the flack, because I'd never done anything naughty before and Mum and Dad would never have suspected I was to blame. I didn't have the courage to own up and I had a sleepless night over that. Janet was seething (and I'm sure she'll be delighted that I've finally confessed after all these years – sorry, Janet!) but it seemed impossible for me to speak up then; I would have gone to pieces, completely, if Dad told me off.

'You're such a bore,' my sister often taunted. She was right, although compared to our Janet it was difficult *not* to be seen as the boring one. She was a stunningly beautiful teenager, crowned Miss Wakefield at the age of 16, and just like our Tony she was very spirited, popular and full of personality. As a young girl I was in awe of their grown-up ways and teenage clothes and friends, but at the same time, whenever my brother and sister caused trouble, I somehow found myself feeling more grown-up than they were. As weird as it may sound, whenever I heard Dad shouting at them in another room I would picture myself sitting on the rim of a soup bowl, watching the chaos my siblings were causing and wondering why on earth they behaved like that. That's how it was every time. I was always the one on the outside looking in, and that's exactly where I wanted to be.

Unfortunately, Mum and Dad were no match made in heaven. They would argue until the cows came home, or fall out and not talk for days. I *hated* any kind of disruption and hearing their cross words just made me all the more determined to keep the peace, and stay away from any heat.

My mother took me to the doctor many times, worried about the fact I ate so little and was so thin and prone to vomiting. Thankfully, we had a very wise GP and he told my mother not to worry about it or force me to eat.

'She's just a very shy child,' he said. 'It sounds like she's just a bit wary of food, but she'll eat when she's hungry.'

When I look back, I'm so grateful to that man. In today's world I might be sent for tests, given medication or even booked in for counseling sessions. And I almost certainly would have ended up with some kind of unhelpful label. As it was he didn't even call me a fussy eater, and Mum just took me home and carried on as we had before.

Sitting around the dining table with the whole family was a daily ordeal for me, though I never complained. Mum had a habit of giving all the best cuts of meat to the lodgers, who were mostly strapping big blokes attending courses at the nearby West Yorkshire Police College. 'You know my rule: "Don't ever skimp on shoes and meat",' Mum always said. Luckily for him, Dad loved all the cheaper cuts of meat Mum served up to the family, like belly pork, brawn, brisket and even pig's trotters. I was the opposite. I hated anything with fat on it and my stomach would turn over as I pushed the food around my plate before forcing down a couple of chips soaked in gravy.

The teachers in my middle school tried to force me to eat the boiled potatoes, meat pies and bullet-like beans and peas served up for school dinners. They told me I wasn't leaving the table until I ate something, but the food was stone cold and congealed on the plate by the time the bell went for lessons and they had to let me go.

'What a waste of time,' I thought, knowing I would never give in. 'What was the point of that?'

Mum was called in, and she explained to the teachers that she had been told by the doctor not to force me to eat. 'Perhaps Jane could bring in some ham sandwiches?' Mum said, as that was one of the few foods I really liked (and I still love a ham sandwich today). The school wasn't happy about this, because nobody took in a packed lunch in those days, but what else could be done? I became the first person at the middle school allowed to take in sandwiches, and a few days later a teacher joined me. By the end of the first week there were eight of us on the sandwich table.

'Good, that's that sorted,' Mum said with a smile. 'There's always a solution.'

It was true that I could always rely on Mum to solve a problem, although unfortunately this one opened the flood-gates on another issue I was struggling with every day.

A group of girls used to circle me in the playground, saying horrible things and sometimes giving me a shove or a slap. The very dark hair I had inherited from my dad was one of the things they picked on. Though Dad grew up in Fife, he was of Lithuanian descent, his parents having met on the boat coming over from Lithuania during the First World War. The school bullies made my life a misery by taunting me with nasty remarks about my jet-black hair, or commenting on the colour of my skin, which like Dad's turned conker-brown in the sun. I didn't understand why this was a problem, although I can see now where these little girls got their ideas from. Many people left Scotland when the iron and steelworks were in decline, and not everyone was happy about them taking jobs and houses across the border, as my parents had. One time, the neighbours on our street started a petition up to stop 'foreigners' moving in. It was a while before I learned who these 'foreigners' were, and it turned out it was us, the McDonald family! 'But we're Scottish!' I exclaimed, the prejudice against us beyond my childish comprehension.

Unfortunately, becoming the sandwich table trailblazer made me stand out even more from the other kids, and that gave the class bullies another excuse to pick on me.

'What you got in there?' the ringleader of the girls said one morning. We were only about nine years old, and when I told her in a whisper that I had a ham sandwich and a scone she grabbed my lunch bag off me to see for herself. 'Plain and boring,' she sneered. 'Just like you.'

With that she threw the contents into the hedge at the back of the playground while her friends started to chant 'Plain Jane, plain Jane' as they closed in on me. The fact I was a very fast runner saved me, because I made a dart for it and just kept going. Learn how to run like Forrest Gump is one piece of advice I'd give to anyone being bullied, because it saved my bacon (if not my ham sandwiches) on many occasions!

It's hardly surprising that every day I'd wake up dreading going to school. I was a bright child, but in order to avoid standing out any further my focus was always on being average, which is what I achieved, consistently. Even in PE I made sure I was only ever third in running races, despite the fact I could run like the wind on my skinny little legs.

* * *

'Here,' Mum said one day, handing me a copy of the *Psychic News*, a paper she and Gran always read.

'What's that for?'

'You are going to sit on this on the coach and then you won't be sick.'

I was 12 years old and this was the last school trip at my middle school, St Michael's. Mum knew I'd been dreading it, and her idea was that if I sat in the centre of the coach, where there was less movement, it would help with my travel sickness.

'Put the newspaper down in the middle seat and make sure you don't sit anywhere else,' she instructed.

Willing to try anything, I did as I was told and could not believe it when it actually worked, both there and back. 'How have I not been sick?' I thought. 'How has this worked?' As soon as I got home I ran upstairs and was sick in the toilet, but that was fine. At least it wasn't in front of my classmates.

Normally I took myself straight to bed whenever I was sick, unable to face even a piece of dry toast, but this time I felt really hungry and went back downstairs. I don't know if I was spurred on by my success on the coach, who knows? But I can remember thinking, 'I'm fed up with this. I need to eat something and I'm not giving in to this anymore.'

Mum gave me a steaming bowl of Heinz tomato soup, which I devoured. It tasted absolutely delicious, and all the sweeter because even at that young age I knew I'd made a breakthrough. 'I've done it,' I thought. 'I've cracked this one, at long last.'

* * *

Looking back, I can see that a lot of my anxiety as a child was caused by fear. I was afraid of food because I was worried about being sick and that was really the root of it all. It was the fatty meat that set me off, but I let that fear grow to such a degree I was afraid of nearly all foods. My tendency to be travel sick was also made worse by dread and fear, and my panic about throwing up in public exacerbated the whole thing, to the point where I was so nervous I felt physically sick before the journey began, even if it was on a push bike. No wonder Tony was flabbergasted by my bicycle sickness. It seemed so ridiculous, but it was fear that triggered *everything*, cooking up a storm of anxiety that played havoc in so many ways when I was growing up.

I still have days when fear and anxiety creep up on me; it happens to all of us. But do I class myself as an anxious person, or a woman who lives on her nerves? Absolutely not. Labels can be very helpful to people who have genuine disorders, but that's not me. That wise doctor had it right.

I have a dialogue ready now, for those moments when I feel my heart sink or race, or when feelings of doom and gloom or worry and dread start to gnaw at me.

'What is it that's making you anxious?' I ask. 'Why are you having these feelings?'

I sit down and breathe, reminding myself that all I have to do is keep breathing and thinking *why I am feeling like this?* Then I think about what my mother always said: 'There is always a solution.' Most of the time, when I work out what it is that's making me feel anxious, it's not half as bad as I feared. And just knowing that makes the solution so much easier to find.

It's been a long learning curve for me, but I know now that how you think about things, and allow them to be defined, is so important, because that has a bearing on how your mind and body react, both to memories and to new situations. Interestingly, when I first started to look back over my school days, my initial thought was: 'I absolutely hated school; all of it.' But that is not true, and writing about it has helped me see that. Yes, I had to contend with my sickness and anxiety on a daily basis, and, yes, I was bullied a lot. Unlike my sickness, the bullying escalated over the years. As a teenager I was dragged into rows about boys I had nothing to do with, which was so unfair and caused me so much trouble. Puberty did me no favours either: mine was not a blossoming, let me tell you. I became the spotty clock with greasy hair, and oh my God the dreaded 'monthlies'! I was so ill with them I had to stay in bed at least once a month, and I was a moody mare, to put it mildly. But – and there is always a but – that is only part of the story. Probably 20 per cent, if that. There's a rule called the Pareto principle which states that 80 per cent of all outcomes result from 20 per cent of all causes: in other words, a small percentage of causes have a disproportionate effect. I think there's a lot of truth in that, and I've tweaked that principle and adopted it into my own '20/80' rule. The rule I live by reminds me that whatever's wrong, it's never 100 per cent wrong, even if it feels that way. Chances are, only 20 per cent is bad, and that's a small amount compared to all the good things that are going on. In times of difficulty you have to look for reasons to be cheerful, because even small chinks of light can help calm you down or cheer up. And they are always there, even if you don't see them clearly at first. It's such a good way to view life, one I wish I'd learned sooner.

When I was seven, Dad was almost killed by a runaway trolley down the mine. He survived with multiple broken bones and ended up taking a much lower-paid job at the pit. As a result my parents sold the boarding house and downsized, and our new home was a small, mid-terrace on Silcoates Street, close to the centre of Wakefield. My sister, then aged 16, was mortified about the big black range and the outside toilet, which she didn't want her friends to see. But to me the new house was lovely and cosy compared to the big boarding house, and I absolutely adored it.

When Mum and Gran had been house hunting I went with them, and in one house we viewed there was a piano sitting in the corner of the living room. Apparently I ran straight over and started picking out a tune I'd heard earlier that day. 'We need to get Jane a piano,' Gran said to Mum. 'Aye, I think you're right,' Mum replied.

In typical style, my father found a battered old piano that was being thrown out of a pub; he could find anything, my dad, and usually for nowt. It had white marks on top where pint pots had been, but it was just perfect for me. Then Mum took on two jobs to pay for my piano lessons, and later for singing lessons too. Just as she'd proved with the school dinner problem, 'there's always a solution', and if my mother wanted something, she rolled up her sleeves and she went out and got it. I'm eternally grateful to her, because the piano changed my life.

'No one is playing the piano in our classroom,' Mrs Brierley said one day. 'Would you like to go inside, Jane, and do some practice for the rest of dinnertime?'

Mrs Brierley was my fantastic form teacher and music teacher at St Michael's. I was nine, and being bullied by a new group of girls, and my teacher had overheard them calling me names in the playground. I didn't need asking twice, and that classroom piano became my lifebelt, rescuing me from the relentless tide of playground bullies. Mrs Brierley had handed me such a precious gift. I appreciated it and was so grateful to her, because playing the piano brought me happiness every single day.

At 13 I moved up to Thornes House Secondary School. I could tell you that it was very rough, it had a terrible discipline problem and that I hated the intimidating atmosphere. All of that is true, but once again, that is only part of the story. The school was in a lovely park, and what a privilege it was to walk through the beautiful fields on the way to school every day. I didn't realise how important that was to me, having something in my day that brought me joy.

I had a key on a string around my neck, because there was often nobody home when I got in from school. To me it was a luxury to come in to an empty house and I *loved* being a latchkey kid. I'd look forward to the solitude, because it was a time when I could sit and play my piano in the parlour, and sing to my heart's content.

Despite my shyness, from a very young age I told anyone who asked that I wanted to be an entertainer when I grew up. I suspect the high calibre of Saturday-night TV when I was growing up in the 1960s and 1970s had a lot to do with it. I adored watching performers like Shirley Bassey, Bruce Forsyth and Cilla, and I would be glued to *Opportunity Knocks*. Still, I'm sure there were plenty of people who thought 'poor kid, good luck with that ambition', because showbiz seemed such an unlikely career for a child like me. Happily, my mother was not of that opinion – far from it. She always felt I was going to do something special with my life, which is why she worked so hard to pay for me to have piano lessons, from the age of eight. Over the years I went all the way up to Grade 7 in the London College of Music exam syllabus, and I took singing lessons for several years too, from when I was around 12 years old.

There was a careers evening not long after I started at Thornes House at the age of 13 and Mum made sure she told the drama teacher, Arthur Starkey, that I had aspirations to be on stage. He sent me for an audition with the music teacher Brian Murrison, who had quite a surprise when he heard me sing.

'Have you been having singing lessons?' he asked.

'Yes,' I said.

'Why didn't you tell me?'

'Why did you need to know?' I thought. 'It's got nowt to do with you!'

I couldn't believe it when he cast me as Dorothy in *The Wizard of Oz*, because I'd have been happy in the chorus, I really would. It gave me such a boost to my self-confidence, especially as I was performing alongside the more senior pupils who made up the rest of the cast.

'Come on, you can do this,' Mum told me on opening night. Inevitably, I was feeling very nervous backstage, but it's Mum's words I remember more than anything. I can still hear her gentle Scottish voice reassuring me, and many years later I wrote my song 'The Hand That Leads Me' as a tribute and a thank you to my mother.

You are the one who makes me sing, who sees the good in everything. Even when I'm low and feeling down, darkness turns to light when you're around. You are the one that leads me, needs me, guides me, loves me.

When I wrote those words, and the title of the song, I was focused on my mother's deeds and kindness and all the emotional support she gave me. It's only now, recalling that night at the school, that I've remembered how my mum used to put her hand on my arm as she offered her words of advice and wisdom. She literally guided me, and though her touch was so subtle, it transmitted the most incredible power.

We all need guidance from someone, and I was blessed to have it from her, all through my life and right up until the end of hers. I feel very strongly that anyone who doesn't have that guidance in their close family should try to find it somewhere, whether it's from a trusted friend, a colleague or an official mentor at school or work. It's vitally important to all of us, not only to help us when we need a lift but to bring out the best in us and to help us reach our full potential.

* * *

The friendships I made throughout my school days were another huge antidote to the nervousness and anxiety I suffered as a youngster, and they are another endorsement of my 20/80 rule on life. I wish I knew then what I know now. We are all different, and there are always people who are brighter and more beautiful than you and exclude you for those reasons. Others will take against you for no apparent reason, or for reasons you can't fathom, but the vast majority of folk are not like that. I was lucky to make some very good friends at every stage in school, great allies like Liz, Jane and Wendy, and though it didn't feel like it at the time, they were a far bigger part of my life than the bullies. My friends were great company and listened to my dreams, and when you are with people you can be yourself and have a laugh with, it is balm to the soul. The bullies moved on – they always do – but friends stick around, some for a lifetime. Wendy went on to marry my brother Tony and become the best sister-in-law anyone could wish for, and I'm so blessed to have her in my life.

* * *

By the time I did my first proper singing gig, in the working men's club in Kirkburton at the age of 16, I'd conquered the intense sickness and anxiety I experienced as a younger child. I'm sure all the positives in my life, including the love of my family, my joy at playing the piano and singing, and the happiness I found with my friends, all played an important role in getting me through it.

I was still very nervous before I went on stage, fretting that I couldn't do it and would let everybody down, but they were normal nerves, not debilitating ones.

'You'll be fine, love,' Mum said, stroking my arm. 'It's going to make my year to see you up there on that stage tonight.'

As usual, she said exactly the right thing, giving me the gentle push I needed.

I took the mic with a trembling hand and started to sing 'Don't It Make My Brown Eyes Blue' by Crystal Gayle. Mum was right, of course. I was perfectly fine once I got going, and afterwards I felt flipping fantastic! Growing up, I'd been to enough club nights with my mum and dad, and seen enough turns, to know when someone has done okay. I got a great round of applause and a few cheers and I was absolutely flying with adrenaline. 'This is brilliant,' I thought. 'This is what I want to do.' It was one of those moments when you feel a cog turn, and you know a new path is opening up in your life. As nervous as I felt at the start, I could do this. I *wanted* to do this, more than anything in the world.

Ever since that first performance, knowing how good I'd feel at the end of a show has helped me cope with my nerves. I vividly remember preparing to go on at the Blackpool Opera House in 1998, in the exciting afterglow of *The Cruise*, and I was absolutely shaking in my stilettos. My throat was as dry as a stick and every nerve in my body was jangling. The same thing was still happening when I returned to Blackpool in 2015, playing the starring role of Grizabella in *Cats*. 'I can do this,' I had to tell myself. 'I *have* to do this, because if Sir Andrew Lloyd Webber believes I can, then I can!'

In truth, I pushed myself every night because I wanted to put on the best show possible for the audience; they are number one, and they are the people who matter most. Even though I started every night quaking in my costume, I knew I'd get my reward at the end of each performance, when I came off stage feeling elated and the audience was buzzing too. And that's the crucial part: ultimately, it's not about me out there. Giving people a great night and making them *feel* something is what I'm there for, and that is my key to facing down fear.

A few years ago, when I said I was thinking of retiring to spend more time with Ed, a lovely fan called Jeni said something to me that explained all of this far better than I ever could. 'You can't retire,' she said. 'It's not your voice, it's ours.' It was such a beautiful thing to say and it really hit home, and nowadays I always think about those words when I prepare for a show. I also imagine I'm flicking an internal switch as I walk out on stage, turning all my nervous energy into excitement. I know what's coming, so I'm prepared to walk through that worry barrier and tell myself: *Bring it on!*

It was such a joy to do that at the *Soap Awards*. As I stepped forward to the sound of whoops and cheers I could feel my nerves fizz and my pulse rise. And then 'click', there it was. The show had started and I stepped into the spotlight thinking, 'Here we go. We were all going to have a fantastic night.'

I was so proud of myself, for everything I'd done and learned to get me there. That anxious child had a hell of a lot of work to do but as my mother knew all too well, there's always a solution. You just have to look for it, trust you will find it and know it will be well worth finding.

CHAPTER TWO

BUILDING RESILIENCE

'How hard can it be?'

'I don't think you'll be able to do this,' Sue said, shaking her head.

I was due to start a tour just three months after losing Ed, and Sue knew exactly what state I was in. I was not only grief-stricken but traumatised, after nursing Ed on my own through lockdown. I was struggling to get through my days at home in Wakefield, let alone anything else. How on earth was I going to cope with being back on the road, performing to thousands of people?

'I have to,' I said. 'I know it'll be hard, but I have to do it.'

Tours take years to come together and this one had been postponed because of the pandemic. When it was eventually rescheduled, starting in Cheshire in June 2021, nobody could have anticipated that Ed would have passed so recently.

'The tickets are sold and I'm not letting people down,' I said to Sue. 'I have no choice. I'll be fine once I get out there.'

The first show was taking place in a hotel that was part of the Warner Leisure Hotels group and people had booked a holiday package to include my concert. This made pulling out all the more unthinkable, and the same was true of several other venues on the tour. There was no way I could upset the plans of so many people who had arranged a holiday or weekend away around my concert. Besides, I needed to do this for *me,* because that's what I've done all my life when the going's got tough. As hard as it would be getting up on that stage, I knew I'd be glad I'd done it.

Unbelievably, fate had tested me in the same way when I lost my mum in November 2018, and weeks later I had a big Christmas show booked at Leeds Arena. Not only was it my first-ever arena show, it was being filmed for a DVD. I had put my heart and soul into preparing for it, not imagining Mum's health would be failing as it was.

'I'm afraid you won't be able to do that concert,' a nurse said to me one day.

Mum had pancreatic cancer and was in the hospice, barely able to speak or drink fluids. I was keeping a vigil at her beside and the staff had obviously heard me discussing the timing of my show. 'No,' a doctor concurred, 'sadly, you won't be able to do it.'

Ed was sitting with us. 'With respect,' he said, 'you don't know Jean and you don't know her daughter.'

Later that day, Mum stirred. 'Don't you dare cancel that concert,' she said in a whisper. Mum was always there to spur me on in my career, and she wasn't stopping now. I wasn't at all surprised. I knew my mother, and however weak she was, the idea that *she* would be the reason for cancelling a big show like this was enough to give her the strength to speak out. I admire Mum so much for that. It took a great deal of effort, in the circumstances.

Just four days later, Mum passed, and something my sister-in-law Wendy said got me through the haze of days that followed: 'You have to live the life that she wanted for you,' she told me. I knew in my heart that Wendy was right, but having her say it out loud gave me the permission I needed to carry on. Two weeks after Mum's funeral, I did what she had told me to do, and I went ahead with the concert.

'If I can get through this, I'll be able to conquer the world,' I told my family before the show. I was talking to myself as much as to them.

There were 5,000 people in the audience at Leeds Arena and I was terrified I'd lose my voice because of my high emotions, which had happened only once before, after

I lost my dad, suddenly and very unexpectedly, many years earlier.

'We've got your back,' Steve Cooper, my guitarist, said. That helped so much. I felt safe with him and the rest of my band around me, but ultimately it was the audience that really carried me through; everyone was clapping and cheering and showing me so much love from the moment I stepped on stage.

I heard a sharp intake of breath when the intro started up for 'The Hand That Leads Me'. I'd sung that song to Mum in the hospice, wondering how I would ever sing it in front of an audience again. My fans knew it was the song I wrote for my mother and I knew it would be an emotional moment, but I didn't bank on what happened next. The entire audience stood up, and then they all started singing along and waving the torches on their phones. My heart was melting and racing all at the same time. At one point I stopped singing and the audience carried on without me. It was so powerful, and I'll always be grateful to every single person there. It was as if they were saying, 'Don't worry, we know what you're going through and we're here for you.' I'm so blessed to have such wonderful fans, I really am. Ed was in the audience that night, in my eyeline, and I just looked across at him, appreciation written all over my face.

Never in a million years did I think Ed would be gone so soon after my mother: two years and four months, to be exact. Nor did I think I'd have to put on another show when my grief was so fresh and raw.

When I got to my dressing room at the Warner hotel, preparing for the first show of the tour, I took a look at myself in the mirror. 'I hope she turns up,' I said to my reflection.

I feel a bit embarrassed to admit I referred to myself in the third person like that, but it's become a ritual that works for me and I'm not changing it. It's something I do every time before a gig now, because really it's a way of reminding myself that I *do* turn up, come what may. When I get the microphone in my hand and the lights go up, that switch will be thrown, I'll start to feed off the energy of the audience and everything will be okay. More than okay.

Considering the Warner holiday crowd was different to my usual concert audience, filled with all my loyal fans, they were absolutely brilliant that night, cheering me on and carrying me through just like the audience at Leeds Arena. I kept it all together until right near the end, when I started to sing another song I wrote for my mother.

The first time I dusted off the piano and sat down to play after Mum passed away, I looked up and saw the lovely portrait of her that hangs on the wall in my living room. It was as if she was looking down on me, which took my breath away. It's quite a big room, and when I put the picture up I hadn't realised Mum would be in my direct line of sight when I sat at the piano, but there she is, in the perfect place to keep a watchful eye on me as I play.

'You're still leading me, aren't you?' I thought when I looked up and saw her. And that was it, the lyrics and the melody came pouring out, making 'You Still Lead Me' the unexpected sequel to 'The Hand That Leads Me'.

I couldn't make it to the end of the song that night. I felt the pain of losing both my mother and Ed, and all of a sudden it was too much to take and tears sprang from my eyes. 'I'm so sorry,' I said, as I ran off stage. Everybody backstage was crying too, but the show had to go on. 'Get yourself together,' I said. 'Come on, get back out there. Show up! You can do it. Just get back out there.'

I always go out on a high with a disco medley, and when I came back out the music had already started and everyone was on their feet, dancing to a disco classic and cheering me on. It was as emotional as hell, but so inspiring too.

'There you go, you've cracked it,' Sue said afterwards. 'Everything from now on will be fine.'

I knew she was right, because Sue is always right (or nearly always – let's not get carried away here). We've known each other since we were in our twenties, working the same circuit, singing in the northern clubs, and she became my backing vocalist after *The Cruise*, when everything went a bit bonkers. Sue has a fabulous voice and could have filled arenas herself, but she was always happier in the background. Our friendship grew steadily over the years, and later she also started doing my hair and make-up and became my PA. Just like my mother, Sue is a wise old bird with laser vision, and I know she has nothing but my best interests at heart.

'Now you've got this one done, you'll be okay for the rest of the tour,' she reiterated. 'Right then, shall I make us a cup of tea?'

* * *

When I talk to myself in the mirror, reminding myself that I'll find my strength from somewhere, I have my mum to thank for teaching me how. She was a living poster girl for the value and benefits of building resilience, and I learned so much from her, not just as a child but right up until she passed.

As a little girl, I'd only had a few piano lessons when the teacher rang my mother with some very unwelcome news. 'You're wasting my time and your money,' she said. 'Your daughter doesn't have a musical bone in her body.'

My mother was indignant, and she wasn't having it. 'I beg to differ,' she replied. 'I think Jane's very musical and I'm going to prove you wrong.'

I was only eight and wasn't bothered if the lessons came to a stop; learning how to play the piano is quite a tedious chore for a young child, and I'd have been happy just to keep tinkling away on my own at home. However, Mum's faith in me was unshakeable and she wasted no time in finding me another piano teacher.

Francis Walker was a wonderful, patient man, which was just as well. I didn't look forward to my weekly lessons with him because they felt so repetitive and the scales were so boring to practise. I was lazy too, but Mum kept encouraging me to turn up and do my best, every single week. Francis was blind, and during the lessons I sometimes made up my own tunes instead of reading the music, hoping he wouldn't realise what I was up to, but he always did because he knew the music so well. Slowly but surely, thanks to Francis' skillful teaching, I started to improve. 'You see,' Mum would say. 'Practice makes perfect. You have to stick at it, Jane.'

I couldn't argue with that, and as I improved I started to really enjoy the lessons. It was a lot of hard work and effort, when a lot of the time I'd have rather been playing out with my friends, but I kept going, week after week and year after year. Francis declared me an accomplished pianist when I finally reached Grade 7 in my early teens. Having the exam certificates from the London College of Music was brilliant, but having a skill that brought me so much pleasure was my real reward.

The bullying I endured at school also taught me resilience. I was in my last year at St Michael's, about to turn 13, when a much younger girl called Julie ran up to me in the playground, crying her eyes out. 'Some girls are after me and I don't know what to do,' she said.

'Which girls?' I asked.

When she pointed them out a fire rose in my belly. It was the same girls who had bullied me when I was younger, and I was not going to let them do this to Julie.

'I'll show them,' I thought. 'I'm not having this.'

When the girls appeared I stepped in front of Julie, eyes blazing. 'You touch her and I'll come after you,' I threatened.

The girls weren't expecting this at all, and they huffed away and never bullied Julie again. That was all it took. I wished I'd stood up to them earlier, but then again, would I have had the guts and gumption if I hadn't survived all the bullying myself? I very much doubt it.

* * *

It was the fabulous Francis Walker who spotted I could sing, when I arrived for my piano lesson one Tuesday night and found him playing 'As Time Goes By' from *Casablanca*. I loved all the old movies on TV, and the radio was on all the time at our house. For a youngster I had quite an eclectic taste in music: as well as being a huge fan of Gladys Knight & the Pips, Dionne Warwick and David Essex, I loved Vera Lynn's 'We'll Meet Again' and the songs from all the old movies, including *Wuthering Heights* and, of course, *Casablanca*. As Francis carried on playing I started to sing all the words to 'As Time Goes By' while a black-and-white image of Humphrey Bogart floated dreamily in my mind. Francis raised his eyebrows.

'What else do you like singing?' he asked.

'Everything!' I said. 'All the wartime classics, everything by Earth, Wind & Fire, all the songs from *West Side Story* . . .'

Francis played a few more songs, including 'Maria' from *West Side Story*, and I sang them all, word perfect. I thoroughly enjoyed myself.

'Well, Jane, I'm amazed,' he said. 'I think you should stop doing piano lessons and take up singing lessons.'

My heart sank like a stone. 'So you think I'm rubbish at piano as well!' I thought. 'That first piano teacher was right all along!' I was terrified what my mother would say, having spent so much of her hard-earned money on my lessons.

'Please don't tell me mum!' I blurted out. 'Don't tell her I'm no good!'

'That's not what I mean,' Francis said, as patient as ever. 'You're good at the piano, Jane, but music lessons are expensive, and if you've only got so much to spend I'd recommend spending it on singing lessons. You've got a beautiful voice and it would be a pity not to develop it.'

When I told Mum she said that after all the hard work I'd put in on the piano, I should do both. 'I'll find the money,' she said. 'Don't you worry about that.'

When my mother wanted something she got it, and she was always willing to take on more shop work to pay for it. I'm so grateful to her for doing that for me, and to both my parents for teaching me the importance of working hard for what you want in life.

I was 13 when I started having singing lessons with Len Goodwin, a classically trained voice coach. Mum took me on the first day – it was quite a long walk to his house from ours – and after that it was a case of, 'So you know where you're going, Jane. Off you go.'

It was scales, scales, scales for the vast majority of the lesson but, by God, Len was good! His wife was an opera singer and she was brilliant too, and I looked up to both of them. After all the scales were done Len would finally let me sing in the last five minutes of the class, and that's when I was in *heaven*. By the time he finished with me after a couple of years I was a trained alto and soprano. Those lessons set me up for life and I'm *so* grateful, because they are the reason my voice has stayed strong through all these years.

While the piano and singing lessons were going on, Francis also taught me how to play the accordion, which I took to like a duck to water. As I improved Francis suggested I join the Wakefield Accordion Band, and at 14 I was performing with them at charity concerts in church halls in and around the town. Dad had found me an old accordion somewhere – of course he had! – and it was a beauty, it really was. I loved playing it and I sang in the band too. I didn't feel nervous at all when we put on the concerts. They were all very low key and local, and I was one of several people in the band.

It was through the accordion that I got that first proper singing gig at 16, performing at the working men's club in Kirkburton. It came about because one of the main players in the accordion band, Wynne, also played the organ, accompanied by her husband, Rex, on drums, and she asked me if I fancied doing a set with them in the club one night. My stomach flipped over.

'What me, just me on stage, singing?' I stuttered.

I didn't think I could do it and the idea terrified me, but when I look back, it's remarkable how easily I was persuaded.

'Yes, we think you'll be great. Just try a half-hour set?'

Wynne said she'd get me some charts, meaning sheet music written out and notated for me, and she also assured me we'd rehearse.

'Right then, I'd love to!' I said, putting on a brave face.

As nervous as I was, I knew in my heart that this was an opportunity I had to take if I really wanted to follow my dreams and make it as a performer. *How hard can it be?* That's the attitude my mother had instilled in me, from as far back as I can remember, and it's a mantra that has supported me and followed me through life.

As I've said, despite feeling nervous when I took the mic to sing 'Don't It Make My Brown Eyes Blue', I got through it and received a good reception from the audience. I not only loved the buzz I felt when I heard the applause from the crowd, I wanted to do it all over again. I look back on that night as such a crucial moment in my career. I stepped up despite my nerves because my dream meant so much to me, and I'm eternally grateful that I did. I'm in no doubt that the various challenges I overcame in my childhood helped me through my set that night. And that's a great lesson to learn: when times are tough, remember that you are learning and growing and building resilience, because the difficult times will make you stronger, and ultimately bring you joy.

My singing career had begun and, before long, so too had my career as an entertainer, though that happened more by accident than design. I was asked back to sing at the club in Kirkburton, and one night someone asked me to make an announcement at the end of my set. The room was noisy, so after saying 'shhhhh' into the mic to get every-one's attention I bellowed, 'Ey up, all you from Barnsley, your bus is 'ere!'

To my surprise, the audience erupted in laughter and when I looked out at all the cheerful faces, it gave me such a great feeling. I loved the fact I'd made people laugh, and that the good folk from Barnsley were leaving to catch their bus with big smiles on their faces. After that I would set out to give people a laugh whenever I was on stage. It was another tool in my kit bag, one that quietly stoked my self-confidence and strengthened my resolve to make it as a performer.

* * *

I didn't become a full-time club singer until I was in my early twenties, having done all sorts of other jobs along the way, including working in two offices, two nightclubs and doing a brief stint as a dancer. I'm glad of each and every one of those experiences. There were so many challenges, every step of the way, and I learned valuable lessons from them all.

The office work, first for Wades Furnishings in Wakefield when I left school at 16, and later as a call dispatcher for a computer company, both taught me what I *didn't* want to do with my life, and there's nothing wrong with that. Neither job was a waste of time, far from it. I learned so many skills besides typing and shorthand, including how to work with other people, the importance of setting aside money for a rainy day (that was all my dad, and I'm very grateful to him for that) and, if nothing else, how useful it is to know how to make a great cup of tea or coffee, because it helps you settle in and make friends.

Working in the nightclubs – Pussycat and Casanova's, both in Wakefield – opened my eyes to the fact I didn't need to have just one job. If I wanted to buy myself a car, I could, provided I put in the hours and the graft. And that's exactly what I did, paying for my gold Vauxhall Viva by working nine to five in the office at Wades, having a quick turn-around and then working in the clubs at night. By the age of 19 I had a TR7, an achievement that made me as proud as Punch.

Pussycat was a thumping pop and disco heaven. I felt right at home there and wanted to do well, and working on the bar taught me that if you were good at what you did you could be a success. Despite being just 17 (this was an era when nobody checked your age or ID), I took my job very seriously, always keeping my bar area and glasses spotless and remembering what all the regulars drank. My reward was a place on the centre bar, which was *the* bar to work on at Pussycat. There the staff launched into pre-planned dance routines whenever certain songs came on, such as 'Oops Up Side Your Head'. Dressed in red leather shorts, a gypsy top and cowboy boots I threw myself into it and worked on that bar every Thursday, Friday and Saturday night. The atmosphere was brilliant and I absolutely loved it.

Casanova's was another level. It was the new, posh club in town and I was delighted when I was offered a job waitressing there on Mondays, Tuesdays and Wednesdays, this time in a brightly coloured body stocking and cowboy boots. There were no security staff in those days, and I soon became an expert in diffusing unwanted male attention with a smile and a cheery 'Now, now, we'll have none of that, thank you very much!' Again I worked my socks off, which brought me to the attention of Janice Craig, who was the wife of one of the owners, Mike.

Janice was interested to hear my ideas about what might work at Casanova's. I told her how popular the dancing bar staff were in Pussycat and suggested introducing podium dancers on the dance floor, which she thought was a great idea. When we launched a new dance troupe called Panther in Casanova's – all the girls were hired and trained by me, under Janice's guidance – I was up there with them, dancing on the podium and having a great time. I was 18 now and didn't have a moment to myself, but that was fine. I relished having three jobs.

A few weeks after launching Panther, one of the other dancers told me she had an audition for an exotic dance troupe in Italy. I offered to drive her to York for the audition and when we got there I helped her rehearse her routine. I'd just had my heart broken by a boy, and when the dance captain who was running the auditions offered me a job in Italy too, it seemed like good timing.

'Why not?' I thought, wondering if I might even meet a hunky Italian to help me get over my heartache.

I can tell you now why not: I was as homesick as hell and we were barely allowed out of our all-female accommodation, which was guarded at all times by an Alsatian dog. I was also put on a strict diet because I was the biggest girl in the troupe, though I was a size 12–14 and curvaceous, and certainly not fat. To be fair, I did look a terror in the outfits. I think having the biggest boobs was my downfall as they made me stand out: the costumes were all sequins and feathers, skimpy bikini tops and little briefs, worn over two pairs of nude tights and a pair of fishnets, so there was nowhere to hide. The fact I wasn't a good dancer probably didn't help matters. All things considered, exotic dancing was really not what I was put on this earth to do.

One night I was so dizzy with hunger that I shimmied down the drainpipe and went and bought a Mars bar. Then I phoned Dad in tears telling him, 'This is not for me, this. I can't stand it. Can I come home?'

'Course you can,' he said. 'Tell me what's what and I'll sort everything out.'

When I got home to Wakefield after seven weeks away, Janice welcomed me back to Casanova's with open arms. First she put me in charge of the VIP lounge, where she would encourage me to sing at the keyboard, and then she got me DJing in another bar, Central Park, something I'd never have put myself forward for. 'You'll be fine,' Janice said, 'Just be yourself.'

I approached being a DJ in the same way I approached being a barmaid, except instead of knowing what the customers drank I learned their favourite songs. 'Here they come,' I'd think, clocking the regular group of rockers approaching Central Park. I could see them in the mirrors before they saw me and I'd quickly play Van Halen and watch their faces light up as they entered the bar.

Casanova's was heaving every night, and the VIP bar was *the* place to go. Pop bands and celebrities staying in the area always came in, and that included huge stars like George Michael and Andrew Ridgeley, when they were touring with Wham! I took it all in my stride, making small talk, serving them drinks and making them feel welcome and comfortable, just as I did with all the footballers and hotshot businessmen who came in to relax and have a good time.

Being at Casanova's didn't feel like work to me, how could it? And that's a crucial trick to learn: in my book, when you do a job that doesn't feel like work, you really have cracked it in life. Later on I started working with the PR team at Casanova's too, something else that was instigated by Janice.

'You've got such a future ahead of you and you don't even know it,' she said.

'Are you for real?' I replied with a laugh, though her faith in me was incredibly welcome and empowering. I felt in my gut that Janice was an important person in my life, and I listened to that feeling. That's so important. Ignore a gut feeling at your peril, I say. It's always a mistake if you do.

My awful experience in Italy had not been in vain. I consoled myself with the fact I'd learned how to be part of a team and do proper make-up and false eyelashes, skills that would serve me well in future. But most importantly, one night when I was dancing round the stage showing too much flesh, I looked at the singer in the spotlight and thought, 'That's what I want to be. I don't want to be this.' It was a moment of clarity. The singer looked amazing; she wore fantastic clothes and the respect she got was immense. I wanted to be that person, so why was I dancing and not singing? What was stopping me being her?

Mum had been telling me for years I had the talent to be the performer I had been saying I wanted to be ever since I was a young girl, and even my cautious dad agreed. 'I have no doubt at all that you're going to be a singer, Jane,' he said.

'And you'll be a brilliant one. You can do anything you want, be anybody you want. You've just got to work for it. And have a plan B. You must always have a plan B.'

He said that to me after one of my appearances with the accordion band, and I never forgot those words. Hard work and sticking with it. I was taught the value of both growing up, and thank God I was. As for Dad's plan B, my answer to that was being 'three job Jane', a moniker I would proudly carry with me as I carved out my careers in TV and music further down the line.

***

They say if you can make it in the working men's clubs you can make it anywhere, and I can certainly vouch for that. When you're up on stage the worst thing of all is being ignored, and when I started working full-time in the clubs at the age of 23 there were some *horrendous* nights when it felt like everyone in the room was ignoring me.

'Second song in, they'll stop talking and look at you,' my mother always said, and she was right, most of the time. I'd say the same thing to any young singer today. Keep your nerve and your belief, and it will all come good.

'Don't expect applause,' was another gem. Other performers often said this. 'You are encroaching on the audience's time and territory – it's their club,' I was taught. 'And never forget, always get off for the bingo, because it pays your wages!'

'Am I actually invisible?' I thought one night, when a group of lads played snooker right in front of me as I sang on stage, cheering loudly and slapping each other on the back each time a ball was potted. I can't remember what I was singing, just the thought that was going round in my head: 'Shall I leave now? Shall I asked to be paid off and go home?'

I kept going, reminding myself not to take this person-ally, and if that's how these lads wanted to enjoy their Friday night in their club, it was up to them.

'Get yer tits out!' a drunken male voice shouted another night, not for the first or the last time. 'Come on, who said that?' I replied, raising an eyebrow and scanning the room, even though I knew exactly who the offender was. 'Let's have a look at you!'

When the lad stood up I paused for a moment then said, 'Oh, I see, it's you,' before giving a disappointed sigh and saying, 'Right, you can sit back down.' The heckle had been diffused, his mates had a good laugh at his expense and I carried on, unperturbed.

I would never have survived singing on the cruise ships if I hadn't done the hard yards as a northern club singer, and

I would never have made it as a club singer if I hadn't done those piano and singing lessons, put myself out there with the accordion band at such a young age or learned so much about working with the public in Pussycat and Casanova's. Everything you do will serve a purpose, even if at the time it feels like you are getting nowhere fast, or don't even know where you are going.

When the BBC filmed me on the *Galaxy* for *The Cruise* I had just made it as the headline act on a ship after eight years of hard work at sea. I was still learning, though, despite being in my mid thirties and with a wealth of experience under my belt. None of us should ever stop learning; if I make it to 100 I'll still have a thirst for knowledge, because nobody ever knows it all, and curiosity keeps you alive.

There's a brutal system on the cruise ships whereby the guests are asked to rate each show they see. If the ratings are bad you're off, and it doesn't matter who you are. I've seen big name celebrities bomb with the guests and that's the end of that; they are off the ship, big name or not.

In my very first show as the headline act, with the BBC camera rolling, I tried to be too clever with my choice of songs and people got up and walked out. It was a crisis point and I had to turn things around, because if I didn't there was a risk I could get fired in front of the camera, and that would be it. Forget just losing my job on the *Galaxy* – my entire career would have been over in a second. *How* to turn it around was the question. The first thing I did was to remind myself that it was my job to entertain people, and you do that by giving them what they want to hear, so I had to quickly re-think my entire set and do exactly that. Secondly, I told myself that this was my dream and I wasn't going to lose it now, having come this far. It was all about looking at what I had to do next, rather than fretting about what had gone wrong. In other words, diving into my reserves of resilience, reminding myself that I was capable of doing this and getting on with it, to the best of my ability. With the help of our fabulous dance captain, Jack Failla, I worked incredibly hard at making my act more appealing to the *Galaxy*'s audience. We changed the choreography and the setlist and, thank God, my next show went down a storm. My ratings leaped up and my job was safe.

With his single camera and tiny crew, the BBC director Chris Terrill was following me and my colleagues around on the ship for a full seven weeks. He didn't film me as much as others, but I really hit it off with Chris. It was all good fun and I was more than happy to go along with it, imagining the resulting footage would end up buried in a late-night TV schedule and quickly forgotten.

None of us banked on what actually happened. In 1998, this type of reality TV had never been done before, and *The Cruise* became a ground-breaking docusoap series, shown on primetime BBC1 over 12 weeks. I will be forever thankful to Chris for giving me my big break, though there were some very hairy moments during filming when I did wonder if it was wise to be quite as candid as I was.

One night I was up on stage, on a high after amending all the problems I'd had with my set, when members of the audience started to get up and leave the theatre all over again. And once again, it was all being filmed by Chris.

What the hell? What's wrong now?

It was not just a few of them either. The holidaymakers started stampeding out of the theatre in their droves. I couldn't believe it; the previous night's audience had loved my set.

'It is what it is,' I thought, my heart constricting in my chest. 'What more can I do?'

I wondered if perhaps this time, the strongest and bravest thing to do would be to admit defeat and make a gracious exit. It seemed the only answer. I'd pulled out all the stops once and how do you do it again, especially when it's all being filmed by the BBC?

There's always a solution.

I knew that's what my mother would say when I phoned her up the next day to tell her the bad news, but surely even she would struggle to navigate me through this latest disaster? I'd hit an iceberg, and a bloody big one at that. Survival seemed extremely unlikely; I was going under, fast.

There's always a solution.

As well as her words I heard my mother's voice this time. It cut through the upbeat song I was singing as I watched my audience scuttling off like rats from a sinking ship.

At the end of the song, someone in the band came and had a quiet word in my ear.

'You what?' I said, gobsmacked.

'Yes, a late-night chocolate buffet, Jane.'

'A late-night chocolate buffet? Did I hear that right?'

'Yes, you did, I'm afraid.'

It turned out the problem wasn't me. Everyone in the audience had gone to investigate a new, late-night chocolate buffet the ship had laid on at exactly the same time as my show. I was so relieved it wasn't my fault, but it was still a crushing low point.

'Sometimes it doesn't matter who you are, how good or how bad,' I said to Chris afterwards. 'If there's a flipping chocolate buffet going on halfway through the show, people will want to go and have a look. That's the reality of being an artist, so you should show it on the programme.'

✳ ✳ ✳

When I had to go on tour after Ed's death, I was grateful to all the people and all the challenges I'd overcome over years – chocolate buffet-gate included – because they all helped put me back on that stage at the Warner hotel, which is what I needed to do. My parents, good teachers and the many cracking characters I've worked with at every stage of my career had all played a huge part in getting me back out there, and with a smile on my face. So too had every childhood bully who made my life a misery, every terrifying new audience and every drunken heckler I'd ever encountered. And let's not forget every sequin and feather that failed to cover my midriff as a dancer, and every chocolate confection in that flipping chocolate buffet!

'What doesn't kill you makes you stronger' is a phrase that came to mind after the Warner gig, and before I'd even had that cup of tea Sue was making I was already asking, 'Where are we on next?'

CHAPTER THREE

NAVIGATING RELATIONSHIPS

'We all deserve to be happy'

When it comes to relationships, they've got a lot to answer for, have men. So too have women, and people of all gender identities, because relationships are hard, really hard. And in my experience, they've been extremely difficult a lot of the time. Looking on the bright side, romances and love affairs may break our hearts, stress us out and turn our lives upside down, but they never fail to teach us something about ourselves, and how better to navigate life and find happiness, with or without a partner at our side.

* * *

Richard Tinker was my first crush, when I was 12 and in my last year at St Michael's.

He was blond and good at sport and all the gorgeous girls were all over him. I had no chance, but I consoled myself with the fact he made my heart leap every time I looked at him. It was a fabulous feeling and one that made bad days at school more bearable. One day I was walking along beside him, my heart fluttering, when another boy came over to me.

'I'm gonna beat you up after school,' the boy said to me, bold as brass.

'What for?' I stuttered.

It turned out this other boy fancied me, and he was jealous that I was walking alongside Richard Tinker, even though Richard was oblivious to my feelings. Suddenly everyone was going round saying there was a fight after school, and so as soon as the bell went that afternoon I legged it out of the gates like a whippet.

'Can I hide in there, please?' I said desperately, after turning a corner and spotting a friendly-looking man standing in front of his garage. 'They're chasing me and they're going to beat me up.'

It was a long way home, and as nobody had seen where I'd gone, this seemed like the safest option.

'Of course, quick get in,' he said, seeing the terror in my eyes and ushering me in, no questions asked.

I was so grateful to the man, but even though I avoided being beaten up that day I was still bruised and confused by the ordeal.

'What the heck?' I said to my female friends the next day, when we discussed what had happened. They all looked nonplussed. None of us could make any sense of it, or how on earth boys' brains worked.

I've never really thought about it until now, but that experience made me draw my horns in even more at school. I was never one for dressing up and trying to compete with the beautiful people, but this made me dress down even more. I didn't wear make-up and wanted no attention at all, whether it was in the classroom, the playground or anywhere else.

It's a pity I didn't tell Richard how weak he made my knees go, because when I saw him years later, when he had obviously found out about my crush, he asked me why I didn't say anything. 'I was too shy, I suppose,' I said. He gave me a pained look, one that made me think I really should have spoken up, because what was the worst that could have happened?

History could have repeated itself when I was 14 and fell for Michael Cornfield, a boy in my year at Thornes House. Michael wore a long coat and had a slight tash, both of which I thought were very cool and sexy. Seeing him kept me going on the days when I wanted to play truant to avoid the bullies, but I never had the nerve to tell him I fancied him. Happily, one day his best friend, Paul, shouted over to my friend: 'Will she be his girlfriend next term?' *Oh my*

God, they mean me! I couldn't believe it, and the answer was yes. Me and Michael hung out for a bit, as young teenagers do. I enjoyed his company while it lasted and it was a lovely time in my life. First boyfriend, first kiss, walking hand in hand everywhere and feeling on top of the world. Ahhhh, young love.

Despite all of this, Michael was so handsome I didn't see myself in his league at all, and spent the whole time reminding myself that this was never going to go anywhere. I can see now that what I needed was for someone to tell me, 'Boys don't care as much as you think they do about what you look like. Don't be so worried! He likes you as you are.' They didn't, of course.

Having looked back on my childhood through adult eyes, once again I can see it was fear that was holding me back, though not without good reason. The romantic landscape was a minefield, and I seemed to be the one who kept stepping on the booby traps. One of the girls in the gang that bullied me in secondary school had a right go at me one day, accusing me of trying to steal her boyfriend. She was furious and making threats to beat me up, and I was so petrified I went to the school counsellor for advice.

'I don't know what she's on about,' I said. 'I'm not after her boyfriend. I don't know why she's picking on me.'

'Have you any idea how bad her life is?' the counsellor replied.

'What?' I said, shocked and confused.

The girl was having a hard time herself, he explained. This was not common knowledge, though clearly it wasn't a secret either, and I was being given this information as a way of shutting down my complaints about the girl's bullying. To my horror, when I came out of the counsellor's office my bully was standing outside, waiting to go in next. I nearly jumped out of my skin.

'If you tell anyone I will kill you,' she growled.

I was even more terrified now, and even less inclined to get involved with a boy – any boy. It caused so much trouble when I wasn't even dating anyone, what would it be like if I did?

Yet another unfortunate altercation, this time at the Balne Lane Working Men's Club, reinforced my dim view of the dating game.

'I know what you're doin' with my bloke,' a girl spat.

Once again I was completely taken aback. I went ballroom dancing at the club with my dad every Friday night and had done ever since I was a young girl. Dad loved to dance while Mum much preferred to be up at the Spiritualist church with Gran, which is how it started. I really enjoyed those evenings. Dad was very popular at the club and a great dancer, and until now Balne Lane had been nothing but a glorious retreat, one that smelled of beer and good times and always made me feel brilliant.

To add to my confusion I'd known the girl who confronted me for years and got on well with her, or at least I did until now.

'What?' I said, knots tightening in my stomach. 'I'm not that type!'

I was 15, and that was absolutely the truth. I was too shy to have a boyfriend of my own, let alone start pinching one from another girl! When I eventually found out what made her accuse me like that, it only put me off boys even more.

'What's going on?' I demanded the next time I saw the girl's boyfriend, or ex as he now was.

'Oh, yeah,' he shrugged. 'I'd had enough of her and I used you as an excuse so she'd break up with me.'

'Thanks a lot!' I said. 'Un-flipping-believable!'

I wasn't interested in boys for quite some time after that. They were more trouble than they were worth, and whenever I went out with my friends it was to have a dance and a good laugh, not to pick up a bloke. No matter how late it was, Dad would always collect me after a party or a night out. Our Janet absolutely hated being collected by Dad when she was a teenager, but it was different for me. I loved the feeling of safety I had when I saw his van pull up, and I think that had something to do with the fact the Yorkshire Ripper was still at large then. I was 17 going on 18 when Peter Sutcliffe was finally caught in 1981, after killing 13 women from 1975 to 1980. Though it was rarely spoken about at home, his reign of terror was huge news throughout that time and I knew all about the fear on the streets, and how the Ripper changed the way women in our area went about their daily lives.

* * *

A rosy light finally came on for me when I met a lovely carpenter called Richard, whose sister Margaret worked with my sister Janet, in Huddersfield. Richard was two years older than me and very family orientated, which I loved, and he had the most beautiful chiselled features and thick brown hair. You couldn't fault Richard in any way, and I fell head over heels in love with him. His family invited me on their holiday to Menorca (my first ever holiday abroad, which Dad only agreed to when Janet invited herself along too) and despite the fact we were never left alone for two minutes, it was absolutely amazing.

Unfortunately, when we got home I found it hard to cope with living in different towns and I was on the phone to Richard all the time.

'Where are you?' I asked, ringing him morning, noon and night. 'Who are you with? What are you doing tonight?' I was a pain in the backside, I really was, and if Richard so much as mentioned another girl's name I wanted to know who she was and what was going on. We split up within the year, and it was completely my fault. My jealousy drove a coach and horses through our relationship, though I couldn't see it happening at the time. Afterwards I was so mad with myself for pushing Richard away because he was such a lovely boyfriend, but at least I learned a big lesson early on. Jealousy is a horrible, toxic emotion, and one that actually harms *you* more than it does anybody else. I've never made the same mistake again.

✳ ✳ ✳

The break-up with Richard happened not long before I did my first singing gig in Kirkburton. I think we all have to make space for good things to happen, and though I didn't plan it that way, I certainly put all the extra time on my hands to good use. Buoyed by my success in the working men's club I responded to an advert in the paper for a singer in a band called the Brian Gordon Sound, which toured lots of working men's clubs all around the north. I got the job despite still being 16 (blimey, I did pack a lot in at that age, didn't I?) and it was a great move.

The guys in the band were all family men who looked after me really well, ferrying me to and from the gigs and always making sure I was safe. It was a fabulous experience and I stayed with them until I turned 17, when I decided it was time I stopped spending my weekends touring the Pennines with these home-loving older men, as lovely as they were. That's when I decided to go into Pussycat to see what the exciting new club was all about, none of which would have happened if I had still being going out with Richard and dividing my time between Wakefield and Huddersfield.

They say that as one door closes, another opens, and the door to Pussycat definitely opened up my world. Cue Mark, the guy who would teach me my next lesson in love, and the hardest one yet. Mark was a gorgeous barman at Pussycat, the type who was dripping with charisma and made your temperature shoot through the ceiling when he came within 20 feet. He was an absolute girl magnet, and when Mark asked me out I was as stunned as I was over the moon. It made me feel special to think that he could have anyone he wanted and he had chosen me. That is, until one memorable night, when another barman, Colin, asked me to go to the cinema with him.

'I can't,' I said, nodding in Mark's direction, 'I'm with him.'

Colin frowned. 'So it's okay for him to see someone else, but you can't?'

It took me a moment to process this information, and worse was to come. When I confronted Mark he just shrugged and said, 'I'm really sorry, but that's how it is. I've never promised you anything.' This was factually correct, but his attitude didn't match how he behaved with me. I'd trusted him completely and I hadn't seen this coming at all.

I was broken hearted and bawled my eyes out at the kitchen table in Silcoates Street, lamenting to my mother how trusting and naive I'd been. I expected her to trot out one of her well-used phrases. 'Don't chase after a man or a bus, because there's always one behind' was one I'd heard her say many times, but on this occasion she was just really sympathetic. 'It's an awful feeling, isn't it?' she said, placing her hand on my arm.

To add to my misery I found I couldn't bring myself to give Mark up, even though it was a stab to the heart every time he was with another girl. I was like a moth to a naked flame, never learning and moving on despite getting burnt every time.

One time I interviewed a new barmaid, and when I asked her why she wanted the job, she told me her boyfriend worked in the club.

'Who's that?' I asked.

'Mark,' she said.

I should have guessed!

I gulped and said nothing, but my day was destroyed. I put her on the same bar as Mark, but I'm not sure what I was trying to achieve, because it upset me every time I saw them together.

As hard as it was to accept, I had started to see that some men are just like that – not cut out for fidelity – and there's nothing you can do about it. It was a brutal way to find out, but you can't make someone love you exclusively if they don't want to. I was second best when I wanted to be number one. I had no control over Mark, only over how I responded to him, and I learned that if you're willing to be second best, then that's what you'll be. Realising that was a quite a light-bulb moment, let me tell you. I also learned that some relationships are just about having fun, and that you need to remember not to fall too deeply as you'll have your heart broken.

I had a moment of sweet revenge when Mark came into Casanova's when I was DJing one night, not long after I'd told him we were finished. He was about to move abroad, so this was my last chance.

'Play me a song,' he said with a flirtatious twinkle in his eye.

'Of course!' I said, fluttering my eyelashes.

Quick as a flash I put 'Gonna Get Along Without Ya Now' by Viola Wills on the decks, turned up the volume and flashed a triumphant smile. Mark was *mortified*.

'I can't believe you did that,' he spluttered.

'Well, I just did,' I replied. 'So believe it!'

Nevertheless, I was the biggest loser, because really my heart was broken in two by Mark. He is the reason I grabbed at the chance to go to Italy with the dance troupe, hoping for a fresh start and maybe a bit of Latin romance. There was no chance of that, holed up and guarded in our all-female hostel as we were. Instead I spent a lot of time in my own company, trying to get over my heartbreak.

Over those lonely seven weeks in Italy I gradually came to some conclusions that helped me move forward. Ultimately I'd had a lucky escape, I reasoned, because if he hadn't been a player, he could have been 'the one', and that's not where my life was heading. 'Whichever way you look at it, you're better off without him in your life,' I told myself.

I felt so much better once I'd started seeing things this way, though it would have been a lot easier all round if Mark and I had had some honest conversations at the start. So much heartache could have been avoided, but I was young and trusting and had no idea how important it is to talk, talk, talk. At least my relationship with Mark taught me this lesson, even if it took me a very long time for the memo to reach my desk and actually stay there!

I had a relationship with another Mark when I was working in Casanova's, and it could not have been more different to the one I had with Mark the barman. This Mark made me laugh, he had a fabulous family and I started falling in love with him, fast. We were so compatible I really could see a future with him, but that scared me. There were red danger signs flashing in my head going, 'Steady on! Settling down is not what you want, Jane. It's not the life for you.' Did I listen? Flipping heck, of course I didn't! I was addicted to this guy and my gut feeling was not getting a look in, at least not for a while. Then one night I asked Mark to dance with me and he refused, and suddenly something in me snapped.

'That's it, we're done,' I told him. 'It's over, for good this time.'

He couldn't believe I'd finished with him just because he wouldn't dance with me.

'If only it were that simple!' I thought. Now I think, 'If only I had talked to him, told him how I felt and let him down gently.' What was so difficult about that?

* * *

'The drummer of Liquid Gold would like to have a drink with you,' one of the owners of Pussycat said one night. 'His name's Wal. Are you happy to talk to him, maybe have a dance with him?'

'Yes,' I said, trying to suppress my excitement, 'bring him over.'

Liquid Gold had had a huge hit with 'Dance Yourself Dizzy'. I had their poster on my bedroom wall and the gorgeous blond drummer had caused quite a sensation on *Top of the Pops* when he wore nothing but a pair of tiny, shiny green shorts and a gold tie. When Wal started walking towards me my heart missed a beat. He was an absolute Adonis in the flesh, and I couldn't believe he wanted to talk to me.

Wal and I hit it off straight away and spent the next two hours sitting at the bar, talking about all kinds of music and having a right good giggle.

'I really like you,' he said. 'Can I see you again?'

'I'd like that,' I said, pinching myself.

It was the start of a wild whirlwind of a romance that opened my eyes to a *whole* new world. Wal was the archetypal eighties pop star, living in the moment and partying like there was no tomorrow. When he took me to a house party packed with beautiful people wearing crazy, outlandish outfits my eyes were on stalks. 'What is this?' I thought. I'd never seen anything like it, though I tried to act cool. Dad came to pick me up at four in the morning, bless him, not batting an eyelid when his ring on the doorbell was answered by a guy in leather cap and a skimpy shorts-and-bib ensemble.

'Did you have a good night, Jane?' he asked, making no comment about how late it was, or anything else.

'Yes, Dad, it was great,' I said.

He didn't ask any more questions. As long as I was safe and he could pick me up, Dad didn't mind what I did.

A few weeks later Wal was off on a tour of Europe, where Liquid Gold had a huge following. After my experience with Mark I had no expectations of fidelity. Wal would be living his rock-and-roll lifestyle, and he would have his pick of other girls when he was touring; I was under no illusion about that. If he wanted to see me when he came back to Wakefield, I decided I was fine with that. In any case, I wouldn't have time to be sitting around pining for him. I was so busy with all my jobs, especially as by now I'd also started doing occasional gigs when the opportunity arose, in various clubs around the region.

Mum was delighted I was back out singing again. 'You've got so much else ahead of you,' she told me many times. Mum made no secret of the fact she never envisaged me taking the traditional route and marrying and having children at a young age. Gran was of the same opinion, convinced from when I was a little girl that my destiny involved a lot of travel. The older I became, the more I listened to Mum and Gran's predictions, and the more I wanted them to be true. Having a ring on my finger and having children in my early twenties, which was what nearly everyone did back then, my sister and brother included, was not the life I wanted or imagined I'd ever have. I didn't know how things would pan out with my career, or where I would travel to, but that was okay. Believing I had a bright, exciting and unconventional future ahead was enough.

Whenever Wal came back to the north I was happy to be his temporary girlfriend, with no strings attached on either side. What was not to like? We always laughed a lot, I fancied the pants off him and I enjoyed the kudos of having a pop star boyfriend on my arm. The summer after I turned 19 Wal called me to say the band were coming to Yorkshire for ten days, and then after that he had a couple of months off before going to Mexico on tour.

'Maybe we could spend some time together?' he said. 'I've just bought a house in Buckingham and I'd like you to see it. Do you think you could get some time off work? Oh, and one more thing, isn't it about time I met your parents?'

It was a yes to *everything*. I was beyond excited. Liquid Gold headlined at Casanova's a couple of weeks later and I found myself sitting with Wal and the bosses from both Pussycat and Casanova's in the VIP bar. Wal was making everybody laugh with his stories and I found his self-confidence incredibly attractive. 'I'll never be able to hold on to this guy,' I thought. 'But never mind, enjoy it while it lasts.'

Wal leaned in. 'The band is staying in a local hotel, would you like to stay over with me this time?'

'Oh, things *are* moving on a bit,' I thought. 'And yes I very much would like to do that.'

Wal was nine years older than me and there was no dressing up he was a man of the world. I phoned Dad to ask permission, and to my surprise his response was, 'Okay, but only if you bring him for Sunday dinner tomorrow.'

Despite the fact Wal dressed for lunch with my parents in a pair of leather trousers and a vest top, his blond hair flowing over his shoulders, he made a good first impression. I think it was rolling fags for Dad at the allotment while Mum cooked the roast that did it. And when Wal went in with the killer question – can Jane come to Buckingham with me, for a holiday? – Dad agreed, though only after a worryingly long pause while he finished chewing his Yorkshire pudding.

'As long as you look after her,' Dad said firmly.

＊ ＊ ＊

What can I tell you about my stay in Buckingham? The house was beautiful but undergoing an eye-watering amount of building work, apart from in the stunning bedroom in the eaves, which felt like a deliciously romantic hideaway. It was our little sanctuary, and what a time we had there!

'Wow, that's a body,' I thought when I saw Wal padding across the room naked in the early morning light. I couldn't get over how beautiful he was, and it was the first time I'd ever thought of a man that way.

We went to parties and I made a lot of cheese on toast, because it turned out Wal was skint, awaiting a royalty cheque, and I had no idea how to cook. On a couple of occasions he took me to look in jewellery shop windows, and we had some oblique conversations about the type of rings I liked, and which one he might buy me. We also talked about me moving down to Buckingham permanently. It was all very thrilling and flattering and I stayed for another week, then another. With the Mexico tour drawing closer, I wanted to know if Wal was serious about us having a future together.

It took Ellie Hope, the lead singer of Liquid Gold, to spell it out to me, one night at a party. Wal was on the other side of the room, drinking and laughing with a crowd of people around him as usual. I told her what Wal and I had spoken about and her face fell.

'You can't do it to him, Jane,' she said reproachfully. 'He's in a very successful pop group, don't hold him back.'

I was shocked by her bluntness.

'What about you?' she went on. 'I can't see you sitting around in Buckingham, twiddling your thumbs while he's off round the world, can you?'

In the days that followed I realised Ellie was right. Even though it hurt to acknowledge it, I had things to do in my life, and so did Wal. There was no *EastEnders* moment. One day I just got up and left, without telling him I was going. We'd had a fabulous five weeks together, but now it was time for me to get back to reality. Wal was gutted, apparently, but he didn't get in touch or try to persuade me to come back. What was he going to say? 'Come back, but I'm off to Mexico and you'll be on your own'?

I missed him like mad when I got back to Wakefield, but I wasn't broken-hearted. My gut told me Ellie was right; it was for the best, for both of us. We all deserve to be happy, and the huge compromises needed for us to continue our relationship would have resulted in a lot of unhappiness. It was another big lesson learned. You need to know when to walk away, and with Wal, it was absolutely the right time.

* * *

My next lesson in love was a huge and quite unbelievable one, because on the rebound from Wal I not only started dating another gorgeous blond drummer; reader, I married him. It should never have happened. Paul was a lovely, lovely guy. We met for the first time when his band played at Pussycat, and we got together the following year, when I recommended Paul and his crew for a gig at Casanova's. I was 21, and I can't explain or properly recall what was going through my head at the time. Was I really on the rebound? That's how I've explained it in the past, but things are never that simple, are they?

I fell in love with Paul, that's for sure. I moved into his flat, 20 miles from Wakefield, and I was that mad about him I gave up my work at Casanova's so that I was home in the evenings for him, when he wasn't out doing a gig. When I look back on the time we spent together, it sounds like somebody else's life. I took a nine-to-five job as a call dispatcher for a firm that fixed computers, and when Paul asked me to marry him, two years down the line, I thought the right thing was to say yes, because I loved him. As Julia Roberts would say: 'Big mistake. Huge!'

We had a traditional wedding at the Spiritualist church, just as my sister Janet had, with me floating up the aisle in a classic 1980s meringue. It was what everyone did then, and despite all my dreams of being a performer, and everything Mum and Gran had said about my future, I conformed. As crazy as it sounds, Paul didn't even know I could sing until I stood up at our wedding reception and did a duet with David Charles, my friend and hairdresser, who had joined me for many a sing-song in the VIP lounge at Casanova's.

The number I chose was Michel Legrand's 'How Do You Keep the Music Playing?' You couldn't make it up, could you?

Paul was stunned to hear me sing, and when we got back from our honeymoon in Spain we set up as a duo and had a good few months doing a spot together at Mr Craig's night-club in Leeds. It was Paul's idea and I was all for it, swapping in my beloved TR7 for a car we could both use and take on the road. It should have been the perfect set-up, but it really wasn't. The shared car was a daily reminder I'd given up my independence, as was the fact that if it wasn't for Paul, I wouldn't even have been back singing. Gran often said: 'Don't think you need anyone else to complete you.' I should have listened. And why had it taken a man to set me back on the right career path?

I'm not blaming Paul; I can only assume my self-esteem was floundering, because for this short period in time I had settled for a life I didn't want. And that meant I had let go of my dream. Like I said: big mistake! Huge!

It took me six months of marriage to admit I wanted a different life and that Paul deserved better too. With my itchy feet and a dream that still needed chasing, I was not going to make him happy, or myself. Admitting failure is hard. I felt a huge amount of guilt when I packed my bags and went back to

Silcoates Street, and four decades on I still feel the need to apologise for my behavior. As far as Paul was concerned it was all fantastic one minute and the next it was over, just like that. I hurt him so much and I feel absolutely dreadful about that. I could have stayed through guilt and duty or the fear of admitting failure, but I know that would have been so wrong, for both of us.

As difficult as it is, sometimes the kindest thing to do is admit you made a mistake and walk away. That's one of the hardest lessons of all, but there are times when it has to be done, because we only get one life, and we all deserve to be happy, we really do.

CHAPTER FOUR

BEING YOUR OWN BOSS

'Know your own worth'

'Why don't you retire, Jane?' Ed said one day. It was May 2020 and we were sitting in the garden, in beautiful sunshine, enjoying lockdown. 'You don't need to keep working. This has been fabulous. Let's just spend more time together.'

With so many people suffering all around the world it seemed dreadful to admit it, even privately to one another, but that first lockdown really had been idyllic. The weather was glorious, we watched boxsets like there was no tomorrow, we cleared out the attic and we were out in the garden all the time. It was a story that was repeated up and down the country, with tired, busy people enjoying being forced to get off whatever crazy carousel they'd been on, stay at home with loved ones and do things they never normally had time for.

Ed and I had been a couple for 12 years, and this was the longest period of time we'd spent together by a country mile. I was a regular on *Loose Women* when we got together in 2008 and I did that job on and off until 2014. I also presented my own TV show, *Star Treatment*, in 2013, but it was from 2015 onwards when things really went stratospheric. Not only was I touring and producing albums on my own record label, but in classic 'three jobs Jane' style I was doing all kinds of theatre and TV work too. It makes me feel tired just writing about it. As well as starring in *Cats* in 2015, I began putting on my own variety-style show in theatres all over the UK; I was also cruising and holidaying around the world for my two Channel 5 travel series and, from 2017, I was the star of my TV variety show *Jane & Friends,* also on Channel 5. Honest to God, I barely came up for air for five years solid, and when I look back on that frantic period of my life I honestly don't know how I did it.

When we met, Ed was the drummer in The Searchers and had been for the previous ten years. He was still touring the world with them, and during the first two years of our relationship we were like ships in the night. We agreed that something had to give and, having enjoyed a long and successful career, Ed made the decision to hang up his drumsticks. There was no struggle; he was nine years older than me and had had enough of life on the road.

'I'll support you in your career,' he said. 'I'll be very happy pottering at home while you're away.'

And that's exactly what Ed did, keeping the home fires burning while I was away doing tours and telly. Now, lockdown had brought us to another crossroads, giving us a taste of what life would be like if I retired too.

'What d'you think, Jane,' Ed said. 'Isn't it time for us to enjoy the fruits of all our hard work together?'

It had been so good just being at home and doing ordinary things and I didn't want that to end. My gut told me that Ed was right; we're not here for long, I thought, and at home with the man I loved was where I wanted to be. I didn't need to agonise over the decision; it felt the right thing to do.

'I'll do the gigs I've already committed to,' I decided. 'But then that's it. It's time for us now. I'll retire.'

We'd emptied out the attic because we were converting the bungalow into a house and we were both looking forward to the builder getting started. It was the culmination of a lot of work and planning over the previous couple of years, and even before I decided to retire there was a sense of us having got our life in order and being poised for the next adventure.

With the retirement decision made, for the first time in my life the future did not involve chasing my career. It was quite a revelation after all the work I'd put in to get this far, but I was in no doubt it was the right thing to do. *Leave the party while you're still having fun*. This was the biggest party I'd ever leave, and I was ready to put my coat on and go, with Ed on my arm. It was a fantastic feeling. I was in charge of my destiny, I had the luxury of being my own boss, and this was *exactly* what I wanted to do next with my life.

* * *

In my early twenties, when I returned to Silcoates Street after my short-lived marriage to Paul, I was ready to launch myself as a full-time club singer. Dad had recently taken voluntary redundancy at the pit and wanted to give Janet, Tony and me a share of his payout. Knowing I wanted a good PA system with a high-quality microphone, amplifiers and speakers, Dad bought me that instead of giving me cash. He also took me to an open night at a club in Leeds, where booking agents came to audition new artists and acts. I got myself two agents that night and the bookings started coming in, and all I needed now was someone to help me on the road.

'Come on, I'll be your roadie and we'll go out together,' Dad said, a twinkle in his eye.

Dad had been feeling a bit directionless after leaving the pit and I needed someone to help with the driving, carry all my gear and generally look out for me in the clubs. 'Really?' I said. 'I'd love that.' It was the prefect solution, especially as I loved my dad's company and would get to spend so much time with him. What I didn't anticipate was how much Dad would teach me during my formative years in the clubs, about being my own boss and knowing my own worth.

'Has it got stairs?' Dad would often ask. 'Because if it has, the answer's no. She's not lifting gear up stairs.' As well as refusing venues that were up a load of stairs, Dad would question: 'Why would you travel that far to do a club, when there's one around the corner for the same money?' If I did agree to make a long journey to a club, he'd tell me to ask for extra money for my time and petrol. 'And be prepared not to go if it's not worth it,' he'd say. 'You can always say no, Jane.'

The main agent I worked with in those days was great at getting me gigs, but he insisted I had to perform for free at the pub he owned. I gritted my teeth and got on with it, because all the acts on his books had to do it, including Too True, a duo of girl singers who were sisters. Their names were June and Sue Ravey, and, yes, that's how I first met my best mate Sue. I went to see the girls perform one night and they were brilliant singers and confident and funny with it. They were also kind, giving me some charts they didn't use anymore, which was so generous and helped me move to the next level with new songs. Sue was outspoken and sassy, which I loved, and we both agreed that the agent was a cheeky devil for making us do the pub for free.

The same agent got me onto something called the Bass Roadshows, which brought me a lot of work and earned him plenty of commission, as at the end of the month he took 17.5 per cent of everything I earned. At least that was how it usually worked, but one night it was a 'pick-up', which meant you got paid on the night and gave your commission to your agent later.

'I think you've made a mistake there,' I said, when the club manager paid me £100. 'My fee's £80.'

'No, you're definitely on 100 quid,' he said, checking the paperwork on his clipboard. 'That's what we always pay you.'

I was absolutely fuming, and my feelings were hurt too. My agent had been skimming £20 off my fee *and* taking his commission, and when I confronted him he had the cheek to tell me: 'If you don't like it, don't do it.'

'Fine,' I said. 'I won't. And I'm not doing your pub anymore either.'

Mum was horrified, worrying about all the money I would give up, but I'd made my decision and I was sticking to it. The next time I saw Sue she told me: 'June and I have refused to do his pub, an' all.' We both had a laugh about it; we were no pushovers, me and Sue, and I admired her all the more after that.

I believe that as one door closes another opens, and I ended up signing with a bigger and better agent, one who helped take my career to another level. I started to win clubland awards for Best Club Singer and Female Vocalist of the Year, and I played bigger and better venues too, including clubs in Blackpool, the Mecca of the north for club singers. It was during this time that an old friend, Vicky Calvert, suggested I become a cruise ship singer, like her. I jumped at the chance – I was always looking for the next challenge and opportunity – and after an audition in London with Matrix Entertainment, an agency specialising in producing shows for ships, I got my first job at sea on the *Black Prince,* which set sail from Tenerife in the spring of 1990.

I was lucky enough to be put in a group with Vicky and two other singers. We were called Atlantic Crossing and were a sort of cruising Manhattan Transfer, and I had a total ball for 12 weeks, sailing the Canaries and having loads of fun on and off stage. I returned to Wakefield feeling fabulous, knowing I'd found something I loved and wanted to do all over again. And that's what I did for the next eight years, singing on cruise ships and travelling all over the world for six or seven months of each year and then doing gigs back home when I returned to Silcoates Street.

I had an initial worry that the clubs might forget me when I was away, but I learned that sometimes less is more. 'When will she be back?' the clubs asked my agent, and suddenly I was seen as a much bigger act, which meant I could pick and choose my gigs. I was earning a good living, although one night I saw the manager paying the men more money than me. I was straight onto my agent the next morning, asking to be paid the same rate as the blokes.

'Sorry, we don't pay girl singers that kind of money,' came the reply.

I was flabbergasted, but all he could say was 'Who do you think you are?' and 'Take it or leave it.'

I chose the latter, telling him I'd do the two shows already booked and then would find a new agent.

'Oh, Jane, don't rock the boat,' Mum said when I told her what had happened.

'Always know your worth, Mum,' I replied, shaking my head.

Unbeknown to me, the manager's son came to watch me at my next show, and afterwards he told his father to pay me the same as the men. It meant my agent had to eat humble pie when he phoned with the news the next day. I never had the same trouble again, and by the age of 29 I was the highest-paid girl singer in the clubs. The money was one thing, but what really made me proud was the fact I stood my ground and did my little bit for women's rights. I encouraged other female singers to follow my example and ask for equal pay. 'There's power in saying no,' I said, 'and when you are prepared to walk away, you are in a position of strength.' Today I would add that it is not rude to say no – it is assertive.

* * *

'She'll be back!' my friends onboard kept saying.

'No I won't,' I said defiantly. 'I will never do a day's work on another ship unless I come back as a headliner.'

It was 1996 and I was leaving the cruise liner the *Century*, fed up at still being in the cast and never having the chance to be the headline act. By that time I'd worked on cruise ships on and off for six years, putting on shows the audiences loved and feeling sure I would do really well as the star turn. If the *Century* wasn't going to give me that chance, my heart just wasn't in it anymore.

My resignation turned out to be timely, because shortly after I handed in my notice I fell head over heels in love with Henrik Brixen. The tall, blond Dane was a specialist engineer who I met when he came on board to work on the ship's boiler. After I left the *Century* I started living with him in Florida, where he had a beautiful apartment. For the first time in my life I was a lady of leisure and I really enjoyed living in the sunshine and not working – at least while it lasted.

Six months after leaving the *Century*, the company that owned the ship phoned me up and asked me to be the headline act on another of their ships, the brand new *Galaxy*. I could hardly believe it; this was a dream come true. I'd be the headliner on the *Galaxy*'s seven-week maiden voyage, and despite the fact I'd be away for Christmas, I excitedly took the job. This was an offer I couldn't refuse. Henrik fully supported me and I have to admit, it felt all the sweeter knowing that if I hadn't walked away from the *Century*, calling time on being in the cast, I would never have been given this chance. You have to take risks in order to progress and, as I've said before, sometimes you have to make space for good things to happen.

Unbelievably, it was just a few days later when Chris Terrill from the BBC called me, telling me that my name had been put forward as someone he could potentially follow in his film. The rest, as they say, is history. If I hadn't known my own worth and taken charge of my career, I would not have been in the right place at the right time, and who knows how my life would have turned out without Chris Terrill giving me my big break?

* * *

It's a pity I didn't carry on making my own career decisions after *The Cruise* aired in January 1998, but I didn't. The viewing figures started at 11 million for the first episode and grew to 13 million, and as the weeks went on the media started to zone in on me. I became a celeb overnight, and when Henrik and I planned our wedding for May 1998, Chris wanted to film it for a *The Cruise* special, and *OK! Magazine* asked for exclusive rights to cover the wedding.

'You'd better get an agent,' people started to say, and I agreed. After all, I was a club singer who'd had a lucky break and I had no knowledge of the media or how the music industry worked. I got myself a London agent who promised to take my career to the next level, and before I knew it I'd signed a record contract and was surrounded by lots of people who were there to 'help' make me a star. Except what they were really doing was attempting to turn me into someone I wasn't. I was told to stop talking and telling jokes on stage; the northern club singer had to go, along with all traces of my working-class background. I was so confused because I was proud of who I was and didn't see why I had to change in order to become a 'proper' singing star, but it felt like nobody was listening to me.

Very soon after we were married, I told Henrik how much pressure I was under to shed the real me, and how miserable that was making me feel. His response was to fly over from America to help, reading the book *Everything You'd Better Know About the Music Industry* on the eight-hour flight. We went straight to a meeting with my agent, and as soon as we left the agency offices Henrik told me he would get someone in to help run his engineering business in the USA, so that he could become my manager.

'Thank God for that,' I thought.

Where do I start in explaining what went wrong? Though Henrik wanted to do his very best for me, he was an engineer with no experience of the music or entertainment industries, and my mistake was handing over so much power to a man who had no qualifications for the job.

The problems weren't apparent straight away. To be fair to Henrik, he did get me some really good jobs and, on the face of it, I was doing well and capitalising on my success on *The Cruise*. After my album *Jane McDonald* came out in July 1998 I entered the *The Guinness Book of Records* as the first woman to have a number-one album without a prior release. HRH the Prince of Wales asked me to perform at a Prince's Trust benefit. I did sell-out tours, including shows at the Blackpool Opera House and the London Palladium, and I hosted the *Star for a Night* TV show on BBC1, which was something I really wanted to do. I had more hit records and performed at the MGM Grand theatre in Las Vegas under Henrik's management, but I was increasingly unhappy, because things were not being done the way I would have done them, and how I thought they should be done.

From the start, one of the problems was that Henrik was very direct, and not afraid to tell anyone in the industry what I would and wouldn't do. The people you work with and surround yourself with are all ambassadors for you, and when it all started to go wrong, my reputation was intrinsically linked to his. Henrik had my best interests at heart, but unfortunately he did manage to rub a lot of people up the wrong way, and that reflected back on me. That was a tough lesson to learn.

Henrik was very bright. 'As a manager, you have to know every side of the business,' he told me. He was right. You have to learn how to be a lawyer, a promoter, an accountant and a whole lot of other jobs, but I had alarm bells ringing from the beginning, warning me that Henrik was out of his depth. I should have listened to my gut, spoken out and changed things and I didn't.

If I had my time again I'd take a closer look at the contracts and I'd be across my finances. As it was I got a monthly allowance paid into my bank account and I accepted that, telling myself I was a performer and not an accountant, and as long as I kept working everything would be fine. Silly me! I lost control of the PR side of things too. Record company execs and television producers were constantly telling me what to do and say, how to dress and how to style myself. I was horrified when a hairdresser cut my hair and gave me what was meant to be a sleek, sophisticated pixie cut, befitting of a glamorous new star. It was just awful, and when I looked in the mirror I didn't recognise the person looking back at me.

My relationship with Henrik inevitably changed. I felt that he started to look at me like a product instead of a wife, and I worried that in his eyes I was always a product that 'wasn't quite there yet'. I still needed improving and embellishing; that was Henrik's mission in life. Sometimes, when I challenged decisions, he told me, 'You wouldn't understand, Jane.' What I *did* understand was my gut feeling, but I failed to listen to it and continued to put my trust in Henrik and all the other 'star makers' in my life. I soon became a very tired and weary product, which was something I desperately didn't want to be.

Everything started to finally unravel in 2001. The BBC had intended to film my Vegas show in the June but pulled out, which was a huge blow and put pressure on Henrik. Then, despite the fact my fans loved it, my record label didn't get behind my latest album, *Love at the Movies,* which came out in the October. If an album isn't promoted well it isn't going to sell; it's as simple as that. Given that you're only as good as your last set of sales figures, the writing was on the wall, and after that album I was dropped by the label.

Henrik was under a great deal of strain but was not sharing things with me. It took a trip to London to see my old friends from Casanova's, Janice and Mike, for things to come to a head. Mike suggested that I might be ready to invest in property, considering how much money I must have made, and he took me and Henrik to see a stunning Georgian house in a quiet square.

'We can't afford this,' I said.

Mike thought I was joking.

'No, we haven't got that type of money,' I insisted.

'Well, you should have that type of money,' Janice said gently.

At last I truly listened to my gut feeling. Something was wrong. Very wrong, and it was time to get my boots on and take charge. My sister-in-law, Wendy, and my old school friend Caroline worked in the posh office Henrik had set up in Wakefield, and when I told Wendy I was coming back home to look at the books while my husband went to a meeting in London, her response confirmed my worst fears. 'Thank God for that,' she said. 'We couldn't say anything to you because it would have been interfering with a marriage and we work for Henrik, but we've been watching what's been going on and praying something would bring it to light . . .'

When I looked at the accounts I felt sick: there was no money, anywhere. I'd worked tirelessly for years, making albums, touring, not to mention presenting a BBC1 TV show! I should have been set up for life with all the money I'd been paid, but there was nothing to show for it. I couldn't believe my eyes when I scoured the accounts. Eye-watering amounts of money had been spent on offices, administration and wages (I had about 13 people on the books), and there were astronomical expenses that I thought had been covered by my record label and production companies. I felt so angry and let down, and I told Henrik I was firing him as my manager. I think he thought I was joking at first, and pointed out that he was my husband, but I wasn't joking. Far from it. I was devastated, and the manager had to go.

It was the beginning of the end for Henrik and me, and we both felt a terrible sense of failure. My work had dried up post Vegas. I had no record company, no TV show and the phone seldom rang. It felt as if the whole industry had turned its back on us.

I didn't blame Henrik. He had done his best, but ultimately he didn't know how to manage me, and I had to face the fact I had been too trusting and gullible, and that if I hadn't handed over so much power it would not have come to this. He went back to America the day after my tour ended in the summer of 2002, and that is when I found myself back home with my mother, licking my wounds and wondering what the hell I was going to do next.

I have no regrets. Everything happens for a reason, and learning the hard way to be my own boss is a lesson that keeps on giving, to this day.

* * *

My journey back began with an appearance on *Loose Women* in 2004. This was my first TV appearance since my marriage ended in 2003, and I anticipated it would be uncomfortable.

What I hadn't expected was being shown a clip of my wedding to Henrik, which completely threw me. I put my head in my hands, shocked at being presented with images of the fairytale that had gone wrong, and then I proceeded to pour my heart out, explaining how my career had come between Henrik and me, destroying the love we once had.

People seemed surprised at how open I was, but without the constraints of Henrik, the record label and everyone else involved in my management, I was free to be the real me. And what a relief it was to be able to say what I wanted, not to mention being free to dress how I liked and have my long hair back. The response from the audience was phenomenal. I was shown so much warmth and sympathy, and it was thanks to that appearance that *Loose Women* invited me back – this time as a panelist.

I'd love to be able to say that my experiences with Henrik and *Loose Women* had shown me all I needed to know about how to move forward in my musical career, but it's never that simple, is it? I took a break from singing for about three years and threw myself into my new job as a Loose Woman, which I loved and was just what I needed to do, not least to pay the mortgage. When I eventually started to sing again I organised and produced all my concerts myself, including a sell-out show at the London Palladium in 2010, with a 15-piece orchestra. It was extremely hard work, but after all that had gone on I wanted to be across every aspect, from selling tickets, booking the musicians and choosing exactly what I wore on stage.

I was offered a tour in 2011, and an agent who had spotted that I was coming back up offered to manage me. He had great acts under his belt, so what could go wrong? Unfortunately, taking on a professional manager/agent was not the dream ticket I hoped it would be. The main problem was that the session musicians we hired didn't seem to want to be there, and appeared to have no passion for making the show the best it could be, as I did. I wanted us all to go out on stage and have a brilliant time, but it just wasn't happening. The energy from the stage is like a big wheel, spinning out into the audience, capturing the vibrations from the crowd and bringing them back to you. At least that's how it should work, but with a sense of stagnation on stage, the wheel just wasn't turning and the atmosphere was flat. Hardly surprisingly, my shows were not the hottest ticket in town.

'Why does this keep happening to me?' I thought. 'This manager has a great reputation and his other acts are doing well, so how has this not worked out for me?'

When I look back, I'm embarrassed to admit that I thought I was in safe hands, not only because I had a professional agent looking after me, but because he was a man. It's how I was brought up. Dad had been my roadie and my rock, and up until this point in my life I had always thought I needed a man in charge. It explains why I had so much faith in Henrik, and that despite the fact I had been performing for 20 years I thought he knew better than me. What a clot!

What I should have been telling myself now was: 'Stop blaming other people when things go wrong. Look at what you are doing. You need to stop thinking men know better than you. They might do, but they flipping well might not!'

Happily for me, there was one man who shone like a beacon of light on that tour. The sound engineer, Martin Hudson, was the one person who really seemed to share my enthusiasm. I knew I was worth more than this, and one night I shared my hopes and dreams with him.

'I know this sounds a bit daft, but I feel like there's much more ahead for us,' I said. 'I can see us in arenas. I don't know if you feel the same.'

'Yes, I do,' he said. 'When you're ready, let's work on it.'

* * *

It was 2013 when I was ready to tour again, and this time I was going to take the reins myself, and I was holding on tight. I brought Martin on board as my tour manager, which is the best decision I ever made. I knew what I wanted, and that the most important thing was to have musicians in my band who respected me and the audience, and actually wanted to be there. Martin not only helped me find some great band members, he cared about every detail, and he worked as hard as I did to put the best crew together. From that point on everything started gradually clicking into place, and my tours started to improve.

Unexpectedly, it was the experience of starring in *Cats* in 2015 that really helped catapult me to the next level.

'Ah, you're the girl who does it all on her own, aren't you?' Andrew Lloyd Webber said when I arrived in Blackpool at the start of the run.

'Yes, but it didn't happen through choice, Andrew!' I replied.

I was playing Grizabella, the ageing Glamour Cat who sings 'Memory' as her plea for acceptance among her old tribe of cats, and seeing how Andrew Lloyd Webber put on a show inspired me to really up my game. Delivering the famous role had boosted my confidence as a singer; I'd had world-class voice tuition to improve my singing range and I wanted my next tour to reflect this. I'd also seen close up how to stage a dazzling production with top quality staging and lights, fabulous costumes, great promotion, and of course a first-class band.

For my 2016 tour, I decided to underwrite absolutely everything myself. 'Let's do it all ourselves this time,' I said to Martin. 'Booking venues, promotion, everything. I want full control this time. I'm putting up my house and under-writing the whole lot.'

'Ready when you are,' he said.

* * *

Being my own boss wasn't half as complicated as I thought it was all those years before: I'd learned that all I needed was a good lawyer and a good accountant, money and the balls to do it. I already had an excellent accountant, and when I'd sat down with a lawyer and explained that I wanted to start to underwrite my own tours, I knew I'd found the right person.

'Good for you,' he said. 'Everybody wants a recording contract, but that's the last thing you need.'

I'd heard it said before that a record label is like a glori-fied bank that takes a high interest rate, but that's not the whole story. A recording contact can be great for artists at the start of their career, because the label not only funds your career, it has the means to promote you and your music.

I'd learned the hard way how tough it is to break even in the industry, let alone make any money. I was two decades into my career and I certainly didn't have pots of money, but I did have a house that I could put up as collateral. That's when I decided to set up my own record label and record my next album under it, and as for the PR, I had a very loyal fan base and people knew me, so I didn't have to rely on a record label to put my name out there.

Martin and my fantastic guitarist, Steve, helped me put together the best band yet, then the manger of the Leeds Grand Theatre, Ian Sime, taught me the ins and outs of the business side of touring and the value of investing in production values. Next, after choosing to retire from backing vocals, Sue agreed to come on board as my PA. I had a dream team at last, one that believed in me as much as I believed in them. And guess what? The 2016 tour became the best I'd ever done.

I was 53 years old, and a whole lot of learning had gone into making that tour the big success it was. I was up and running like never before, and that was when Ben Frow, the director of programmes for Channel 5, asked me to present a cruise ship travel show and sing a song at the end of it.

'Let's do it!' I said. I clicked with Ben straight away. He's hugely talented and enthusiastic and I instantly knew I could work really well with him. To be truthful, though, I wasn't sure about singing the song at the end. Would it be cheesy? Would I be a disaster as a travel show presenter?

You know what, Jane? Give it a go, but remember this. Don't hand over your power and remember what you are worth.

My newfound TV career had begun. All the lessons I'd learned over the previous (gulp) 30 years undoubtedly helped me not only survive but make the most of the crazy but brilliant four years of work that followed, leading me to the point in lockdown when I was ready to pack it all in and retire with Ed.

Once that decision was taken I had an answer for anyone who questioned me, and no, it wasn't simply that I was leaving the party while I was still having fun. 'I'm my own boss,' I said. 'I haven't always been in charge of my own life, but I am now, and I'm making the most if it.'

LEARNING FROM FAILURE

'Trust in the future'

Would I still be living in Florida with Henrik, had the BBC not turned up on the *Galaxy* and made *The Cruise?* Not surprisingly, it was a thought that went through my mind as I hid away, back home with my mother, in the miserable months that followed the breakdown of our marriage.

Henrik and I had a year together before the docusoap was screened, and what a wonderful time that was. I liked the look of him as soon as I was introduced to him on the *Century,* and we ended up spending the next two weeks stealing kisses in dark corners and sneaking in and out of each other's cabin. Relationships between people working on the ship were frowned upon, but I couldn't help myself. I hadn't had a serious relationship in years, and Henrik ticked every box: not only was he tall, blond and handsome, he had a great job and was ambitious with it. People saluted him as he walked on and off the ship, and the power he had made me fancy him even more. I was besotted with him after our first fortnight together and, though Henrik was not a demonstrative person, the feeling appeared to be mutual because after that the *Century*'s boiler seemed to be on the blink an awful lot!

Once a week the ship docked at Fort Lauderdale, where Henrik was based, and if he wasn't working he would be waiting for me on the quayside. It wasn't long before I was invited back to his apartment – a Scandi-style bachelor pad, in a modern block with a private pool. It was *bliss* swimming in the sunlit water, surrounded by rustling palm trees and sweet-smelling flowers. This could not be further away from the world I knew back in Yorkshire, I thought. *How am I here?*

I was asking myself the same question when we got married on the paradise island of St Thomas in the American Virgin Islands. Granted, we could have done without the film crew and magazine journalists being there, which made it feel more like a job than a wedding, but the setting was *idyllic* and I had to pinch myself that this was real. Here I was on a tropical beach, in a beautiful designer dress, marrying my gorgeous Danish man. I was on cloud nine when Henrik put the ring on my finger, and the fairytale would continue after the wedding, because I had my soaring career to fly back to.

Less than four years later, alone in my bedroom in Wakefield, I found myself struggling to come to terms with how I was back *here*, my life with Henrik now just a series of memories, some amazing, others quite the opposite. I felt a complete failure. Everything had come crashing down around my ears, and things could not be any worse. I was getting divorced, I had no work and I was financially ruined. And when I say ruined, I really mean it. Not only had I lost all the money I'd ever earned, it turned out I owed considerable sums to the taxman too. I was absolutely broken, and I had no idea how to put myself back together.

When things unraveled with Henrik we parted company very quickly. My career had crashed and burned on his watch and the sooner he was gone the better my chances of survival in the industry. He knew that, and he left the day after I did the last concert at the end of my 2002 tour. I didn't feel any malice towards Henrik and I didn't want anything from him. He wanted to go back to America and live his own life and I guess I loved him enough to just let him go, and to wish him well in the future. At the end of the day, he had done his best and it didn't work out for us. What more can you say? There was no point in getting bitter and resentful about it, that's not for me. It's better to let people go with a good heart and

I wanted to look forward not back. I'd just have start again, and do it on my own this time.

I started to think I would probably have to go back on the ships, which I really didn't want to do, but what choice did I have? At least I had that option if I wanted it. Dad would have been proud, I thought. I wasn't exactly 'three jobs Jane' at the minute, but at least I had a plan B I could fall back on.

Eventually one job offer did come in – playing the nurse in a new West End production of *Romeo and Juliet: The Musical*. I should have been delighted. It was a great opportunity for me, but I still felt so low after Henrik that I couldn't face doing it. I told my sister-in-law I was turning it down flat: I wasn't ready to face my neighbours in Wakefield, let alone start singing on a West End stage. Wendy blanched. 'You have to take the show, Jane,' she said. 'You're in so much debt, and you've got a tax bill coming in.' It was a horrible reality check, but Wendy was right and I had to listen to her.

Thankfully, the part of the nurse turned out to be perfect for me, because I had to cry over Juliet every night and sometimes I genuinely sobbed my heart out, which did me some good, I think. I earned enough to clear my debts and working in London with a great cast brought me out of myself.

However, once the run was over and I was back home with my mother, reality dawned again. Sorting out the divorce was the only thing in my diary, and I shut myself away, feeling lower than ever.

* * *

When he became my manager Henrik made it plain he wanted us to live in London together, but I'd been away from home for long enough over the years and I insisted I wanted to be in Wakefield near my friends and family. I'd have been very happy living with my mother in Silcoates Street, and I tried to convince Henrik it would make the perfect base for us. 'We're going to be working away a lot, and touring,' I argued. 'When I've been on the road I don't like to come into a cold house. I like to come into a home where there's a warm welcome and the smell of cooking. Mum will love it too. Let's just stay with her? It's a win-win.'

Henrik wasn't sold on the idea, and who can blame him? He persuaded me to buy a bigger house nearby, in Howcroft Gardens, and I went along with it on one condition: we sold Silcoates Street and my mother came to live with us. It took a bit of persuading, but both Henrik and Mum agreed to the plan. Getting rid of Mum's old furniture was quite a challenge. For instance, she still had our big old Edwardian dining table from the boarding house in Eastmoor Road, but that wasn't going to fit into our modern new home, which Henrik decorated in the same minimalist style as his Florida apartment. It was all a massive change for Mum, but she got on board and let her old stuff go. It turned out to be a great move for her; Mum loved having everything new, including her own en suite, and from my point of view it really was a comfort to come home to a cosy home and a pie in the oven after being on the road for weeks on end.

Little did any of us know how short-lived this arrangement would be, and that it would end up with just me and Mum living together in Howcroft Gardens when my marriage ended. But things happen for a reason, and I thanked my lucky stars I had Mum there when I hit rock bottom because, by God, I needed my mother.

When you've fallen off a pedestal you just want to hide away, but Mum always made sure I got up and had something to eat in the morning, even if all I did after that was to wrap myself in a duvet and sit on the sofa, crying and watching TV. I was like that for months on end, with Mum keeping a watchful eye on me, and then one day an old friend called in to see me. He didn't know what had gone on and was shocked at the state of me.

'Oh God, what's happened?' he asked.

'I'm done with the music industry,' I said. 'I'm never going back to it. I don't even want to listen to music anymore.'

My friend had never seen me like that, and he dished up some tough love that day. Knowing I had a big mortgage on Howcroft Gardens, he pointed out that if I didn't go back to work I'd lose the house.

'I can live in a caravan,' I sniffed. 'That'll be fine for me.'

Just at that moment Mum came in with a tray. 'Here we are,' she said in a sing-songy voice. 'There's nothing a cup of tea can't fix.'

I looked across at my friend, and it was as if he read my mind: *I can't do that to my mother. She is not losing her home, no way.*

It was the wake-up call I needed. I'd got myself stuck in a cycle of asking myself why I had been treated so badly and blaming others for my failure. It wasn't just Henrik who'd let me down, I was blaming so many people in the industry. This had to stop, I realised. I needed to take responsibility for my downfall, because *I* was the common denominator in everything that had gone wrong.

Get a grip, Jane. It's up to you.

I wasn't sure how, but I knew I had to pull myself together, somehow. I used to watch QVC all the time, and shortly after my friend came round I saw an advert for Tony

Robbins' self-help book, *Unlimited Power: The New Science of Personal Achievement.*

'You've got nowt to lose,' I thought, sending off for it. It turned out to be really helpful, full of positive messages and advice, and reading it reminded me that I needed to stop being a victim and start being who I wanted to be, and living the life I wanted for myself.

Still, it was a struggle to put this good advice into practice.

'Can you come and help me with the shopping?' Mum asked one day. 'I'm going to the butcher's and I can't carry all the bags.'

I hadn't stepped foot out of the house in months. It was the last thing I wanted to do, because what did people know, and what would they think? I was sure everyone would be looking at me, carrying a blinking bag of meat, thinking what an utter failure I was.

'I can't do it,' I said. 'Don't make me!'

But Mum wasn't letting me off the hook. 'I need your help, Jane,' she insisted. 'Please help me, I won't be able to manage.'

I'm so glad she persisted.

'Hiya, love!' neighbours said, when I passed them in the street.

'Oh, hi!' I said nervously.

'Hello Jane!' the staff in the butcher's said.

They had smiles on their faces and they were being nice to me, just as they always had been. It was a huge lesson. You can't predict what other people are thinking and you mustn't project your own thoughts onto others, because you'll probably get it wrong. That short shopping trip also showed me the importance of pushing yourself out of your comfort zone. When you do, you will be rewarded, and things will get better. Or at least they have a greater chance of getting better than if you stay wrapped in your duvet in front of the telly.

From that day on, I slowly began to get better. I started going swimming every morning, doing twenty lengths. Reading Tony Robbins and another self-help book, *Excuse Me, Your Life Is Waiting: The Astonishing Power of Feelings* by Lynn Grabhorn, helped motivate me. I learned that if I went swimming, whatever else I did I'd already had a success first thing in the morning, which improved my mood and motivated me for the whole day. I also began to listen to music again, and it must have been around this time when 'Let the Light In' was gradually taking shape in my head.

Writing that song was such a positive step. 'What is it in this world you really want?' I asked myself. Through my music I was telling myself to keep following my dreams, and to keep looking for the next happy ending. I wanted to be happy again. *All* of us want to be happy, and in the end I hadn't been happy with Henrik. You can't make someone love you when the love has gone, and I could see in Henrik's eyes that his love for me had gone. It was heartbreaking but true, and being honest with myself about that was so helpful. Ultimately, if you are with someone who makes you unhappy that is a very long and wasted life. Henrik and I had stopped bringing each other happiness, and we both deserved better. When I accepted that I started to feel so much better about everything. There were no regrets and recriminations, just sadness. I felt the same way about the business side of things. If I harked back to how much money I'd lost I'd tear myself apart, even today, but why put myself through that?

* * *

Given that my parents argued like cat and dog, I can remember once asking my mother why she stayed with my dad. It seemed baffling to me that they plodded on year after year, because they had so little in common and didn't seem to bring each other joy. I was quite young at the time, and Mum's answer has stayed with me. 'Where would I go?' she said, and it was so sad to hear her say that. It was a different era then, of course. Working-class women, and especially mothers, soldiered on because they had precious little choice. 'You've made your bed now lie in it' was the attitude that prevailed. I'm so grateful times have changed, though I appreciate that even in this day and age it's very hard to leave a marriage. It's no surprise the divorce rate in England and Wales is at a 50-year low while we are in a cost of living crisis, and for many people my mum's question – 'where would I go?' – is still a big barrier to breaking away.

There are some people who don't want to leave, even when the marriage has broken down beyond repair, and I don't blame anyone for staying in a life they have worked so hard to achieve. When things go wrong, walking away from your home and everything you have spent years building up seems unthinkable, and impossible. But nothing is impossible. You have to consider this: is it really worth staying in a life that does not fulfill your happiness in any way, shape or form, or are you willing to walk away, start again and take half of the life you have built up? If you do walk away, and even if you walk away empty-handed like I did, I can promise you there is a whole world out there, full of different opportunities and new chances of finding happiness. There's an American ultramarathon runner called Dean Karnazes who once said, 'Sometimes you've got to go through hell to get to heaven.' It's a great belief to hold on to, because one thing is certain: if I had never met Henrik and failed in so many ways, I wouldn't be where I am today.

Focusing on positive thoughts was one of the things that helped me move forward after the split. Before I met Henrik I'd spent years on my own, on and off, and I often reminded myself that I was good at being single and looking after myself. I thought back to one of the best holidays I ever had, when I went on a solo trip to Venice, during my time on the ships. I flipping loved it. I loved that I could walk when and where I wanted, at my own pace. I sat and had a Bellini in Harry's Bar and a coffee in St Mark's Square, watching the world go by, and that was fabulous. The temperature was lovely, and through the open window of my beautiful hotel room I could hear music playing. 'This is heaven,' I thought. I didn't need a man there, I was more than happy on my own. It's amazing how helpful positive thoughts can be.

✻ ✻ ✻

As I've already said, I wish I could say that my experiences with Henrik as my manager taught me how to avoid making the same mistakes over and over again in business, and in my career. They didn't, unfortunately, and the same is true in my personal life, because after Henrik I still had some big lessons to learn about love and relationships.

Once I was properly back on my feet and solvent again, I took my mother on a cruise to the Seychelles, to thank her for all the support she had given me. I did a lot of thinking while we were there, and one evening I got talking to a well-known psychologist who was onboard. Coaxed along by my mother, I ended up telling him everything about how I'd been married twice, and how relationships never seemed to work out for me. 'The problem is you're picking all the wrong men,' he said, 'and you're following the same pattern again and again. You need to go for someone completely different.' He concluded that I was attracted to powerful men who were drawn to my vulnerable side, and that when they tried to take control I fought it. *Wow.*

I revised my checklist. I still wanted a good-looking bloke, but powerful and successful? Not anymore – I'd been there, done that and worn the T-shirt. Above all, what I really needed was man who was kind and loving and didn't need to be in charge.

Jarek Pyc was the sax player in the band on our cruise ship, and I first noticed him because he was a really talented musician. He wasn't my type – he was dark-haired and not as tall as the men I usually went for – but he was a good looker all the same. 'He's a bit fit,' I said to someone in the group we were sat with. Two of the men I was chatting to were gay. 'I think he's one of us,' one of them said cheekily. 'He's not gay!' I laughed. And let's just say that during the course of that cruise I found out that Jarek wasn't gay, and the pleasure was all mine in proving my friends wrong!

I also learned that Jarek was 12 years younger than me, and he was gentle and kind by nature. He was just the ray of sunshine I needed in my life. Let's be honest, we all want to be liked and we all want to be loved, and when your marriage has failed you want to see if you can still pull. Jarek and I enjoyed a lovely holiday romance that spilled over into real life. When you've not had love for a long time it's addictive, and Jarek was really helping me to heal after my divorce. A short time after the Seychelles cruise ended I went to meet him in Venice, on another cruise ship he was working on, and then I asked him if he wanted to come to England, to work with me.

'Do you fancy a job, in my band?' I said.

'Er, yeah,' he said tentatively. 'I didn't know you were in a band.'

I hadn't mentioned I was a singer, and when Jarek Googled me he was quite surprised by what he found. I explained that I was just starting up again, with plans to play in small venues. Sue had got me going on this. 'Whatever you've been through, you're still a singer,' she told me, one night over a drink. 'Nobody can take than from you.' Sue knew a promoter who was keen to offer me a mini tour, and even though I felt nervous about taking this step, I had agreed to give it a go. You have to keep growing, I told myself. This was not going to be easy, but doing nothing would make me feel a lot worse. I recognised that I needed to feel safe and surrounded by people who cared about me, and Sue was going to be my senior backing vocalist. Having Jarek beside me too would be fantastic, I thought, and as soon as he'd finished his contract on the ship, he came to stay with me in Wakefield.

My mother was mortified. 'What are you thinking?' she said. 'You're going out of the frying pan, into the fire.'

'I'm not marrying him!' I said. 'It's just nice to have a boyfriend again, and he's a good person, and a great sax player!'

Things started off well. My first concert on that tour was at the Wolverhampton Grand Theatre, in the autumn of 2003. Despite all the famous venues I'd played in previous years, this suddenly felt like the most important gig of my life. I was petrified backstage, but when I came out and saw the familiar faces of my fans in the crowd my fears and insecurities melted away. It was like coming home, and I was so relieved and thankful to the fans and everyone who was surrounding me with love that night, including Sue and Jarek and all the people in the audience.

It felt like Jarek was the right person for me at the right time in my life. I was in love and everything was rosy in our relationship, and I promoted him from sax player to my MD. We'd been together for more than a year by that time, on and off, but then things started to go wrong. In hindsight I can see that I'd grown and moved forward in my life, and I knew I was going to keep on growing, because that's how I am. Jarek didn't share my hopes and dreams, and that's fine. He was still a good person and a kind man, but he had different ambitions and it wasn't going to work between us anymore.

Unfortunately, the end of our relationship impacted on the atmosphere on stage. It's never easy breaking up, and I think Jarek was shocked that I called it the way I did. I can't hobble on when a relationship has gone wrong and as soon as I realised we'd come to the end of our road together I cut loose very quickly. The disruption and upset this caused between Jarek and me seemed to infect all the musicians, and when I went out on stage I felt like I was on my own, with absolutely no support. Sue was very worried about me, and rightly so. Things had gone pear-shaped once again, but at least I'd learned a valuable lesson. 'I am never, ever mixing business with pleasure again,' I told Sue. 'It never works. What was I thinking?' Sue, bless her, resisted the urge to ask me how the hell I hadn't learned that lesson with Henrik.

Though I should never have brought my boyfriend into my band, I don't regret my relationship with Jarek. All told we were together for about two years. We had a lot of fun for most of it, and afterwards I was left with the precious knowledge that I was *never* going to make the same mistake again.

* * *

Happily, when I met my true love, the valuable lessons I learned from every one of my failed relationships were in my locker, ready to help me make this one work. I'm so grateful for that, because if I'd met Ed at a different time in my life, when I didn't have the wisdom I'd accumulated over the years, it wouldn't have worked out between us. I can say this with certainly, because I actually did meet Ed many moons earlier, at a point in our lives when we weren't ready to settle down together.

'I used to go out with him!' I told Donna, the make-up artist on *Loose Women*.

She followed my gaze to the TV monitor in the dressing room. The Searchers were on *This Morning*, talking about their new album, and the drummer looked every bit as handsome as I remembered him.

'You've got to go and say hello,' Donna said.

'I can't do that,' I said. 'He's probably married with kids.'

'It doesn't stop you saying hello, does it?'

Donna dragged me to the *This Morning* studio, my heart going like the clappers.

'Hello, do you remember me?' I said.

I was frightened Ed wouldn't recognise me, but his face lit up. 'Oh, he's still lovely,' I thought.

'Jane!' he said, picking me up and swinging me around. It was such a lovely reaction, and even the rest of the band went, 'Ah!'

That were it; me and Ed were together from that moment on. There was a lot to catch up on, because 26 years had passed since we first hooked up. For one thing, the last time we were together, his name wasn't Ed, it was Wal. And instead of being a dashing, middle-aged member of The

Searchers, he was the party-loving drummer in Liquid Gold – yes, that same crazy eighties pop star who rolled fags for my dad at his allotment, whisked me to his pad in Buckinghamshire and then jetted off to Mexico to sing 'Dance Yourself Dizzy' to screaming fans.

He told me he had started using his middle name of Ed because two other members of The Searchers were called Frank and Spencer, and to have a Wally alongside those names was too ridiculous. Being old enough to remember the hapless, accident-prone Frank Spencer in the 1970s sitcom *Some Mothers Do 'Ave 'Em,* I knew exactly what he meant, and it made me laugh. Ed also told me his decree nisi had just come through. Talk about timing, I thought. I'd been single for quite some time, and the spark between us was definitely still there. Ed was as charming and funny as I remembered him, and we had a great laugh reminiscing about the old Pussycat days, and that memorable Sunday roast with my parents, when Dad gave his permission for me to stay with Ed at his house in Buckinghamshire.

'I'm going to take you for dinner and a show,' Ed said, after I agreed to go on a date a few weeks after we were reunited. What he actually did was take me for a hotdog and to watch The Searchers, as he was working that night.

'That's my kinda guy!' I thought.

I was so proud watching him perform. He was a brilliant drummer, and before I knew it all my old feelings started coming back. It was like being a teenager again, watching Liquid Gold: Ed was bloody gorgeous and I fancied the pants off him. It made no odds that they were sensible black trousers now instead of shiny skin-tight disco pants – after all, I was in a silk shirt and tailored slacks instead of a gypsy top and red leather shorts!

It's unusual for me to fancy blokes. That instant 'phwoar!' reaction rarely happens, and I think that's why I'd been single for a while. My mother always said: 'Don't chase after a man or a bus, because there's always one behind.' I listened to that advice when I was younger and, as I got older, I learned not to chase feelings either. If that instant spark isn't there, in my book it isn't worth bothering. With Ed, not only was the chemistry there, he was also an all-round great person.

'Tell me about this bloke you've met,' Sue said. 'What's he like?'

'Oh, he's just lovely,' I said.

'Oh,' Sue said, taking a sharp intake of breath. 'That's dangerous.'

I knew exactly why she reacted that way. Normally when I told her about a new man it was all about the excitement of where he was taking me or what we were doing, but there was none of that this time. Ed was just lovely. We were meant to be together; that's how it felt from the start.

Unfortunately, we had our work cut out to make our relationship work. With Ed still touring the world and me away a lot, singing and performing and doing *Loose Women*, it wasn't easy to spend time together. Still, my gut was telling me we really had to make this work this time, despite the challenges, and happily Ed felt the same way.

We'd only been together for a few months when Ed proposed on Christmas Eve 2008, at our local Italian restaurant. I was so surprised and overwhelmed that I started crying. People in the restaurant thought he'd broken up with me and I started laughing when I saw their horrified faces. 'No, it's okay,' I said, laughing. 'He's just asked me to marry him.'

Though I went home with an engagement ring on my finger that night, ultimately Ed and I never married. I thought long and hard about it, and in my heart I didn't think we needed to. 'Let's wear the rings but stay as we are,' I said. 'We'll always be here because we want to be, and not because we have to be.'

Ed agreed, and it was a very good decision. We were so happy as we were, and why complicate things? Though we didn't have a wedding we went on loads of 'honeymoons', to places like the Maldives and Venice, and that was plenty enough for us. Most importantly, when we were at home we sat on the sofa like two peas in a pod, talking and laughing for hours, about everything under the sun.

I'd recently moved into a bungalow with my mum, which is where I still live today. She'd spotted it in the local paper and told me if she won the lottery she'd buy it. It was in a great location and I could afford it, so I bought it, not long before I met Ed. Funnily enough I've never picked a single one of the homes I've owned, but Mum had chosen well, and when Ed moved in with us the set-up worked really well. There was enough space for everyone and it never felt like three's a crowd, not least because Ed and me we were both working away so often. Meanwhile, Mum always kept herself busy, going out and about with her friends and doing what she'd done for years, running the house like clockwork and cooking lovely meals. When Ed decided to retire, two years down the line, I hadn't really thought about how we'd all manage the change, but thankfully Sue had.

'I hate to be the bearer of bad news,' Sue told me straight one day, 'but if you want to keep Ed, you're gonna have to move your mother out.'

We were on a trip to Marbella, and I can remember the moment very clearly.

'What?' I said, giving a little shiver in the sunshine.

I'd lived with my mother for so long I couldn't imagine us living apart, but my gut told me to listen to Sue, and listen I did.

'You know I love your mum,' she said, 'but she's the matriarch and she doesn't want anyone to come between you and your career.'

This was undeniably true. Mum had got rid of quite a few boyfriends in the past, not directly but by planting seeds of doubt and steering me in the direction she thought was best.

'You can't go on like you have been,' Sue went on. 'Your mum will come between you and Ed, and this one's a keeper. Take my advice and buy your mother another house.' It wasn't what I wanted to hear, but I felt the wisdom in Sue's words, and I trusted in them.

To my surprise, when I got home it was Mum who broached the subject, and she had obviously got a little speech prepared in her head.

'Now he's retiring, this is not gonna work, with Ed and me,' Mum said.

'You're right,' I replied, relieved she'd started the conversation. 'Let's buy you a place nearby.'

Mum's face was a picture of shock, and I was taken aback too, because that's when I realised we were coming at this from completely different angles. My mother thought I was going to say: 'You're right, Mum, Ed's gonna have to go', but that was not the case at all. I felt awful and started to question whether I could go through with it, but Sue and my sister-in-law, Wendy, weren't having it, and they encouraged me to stick to my guns. 'Your mum needs her own life as much as you do,' Wendy said, which was exactly the right thing to say. I hadn't looked at it that way, and that helped spur me on as I took Mum house-hunting and helped her settle in a lovely new bungalow around the corner from ours. She really loved it, in the end. I could pop in every day and it was so much better for everybody. It even brought me and my sister Janet closer. She could never understand why I lived with our mother for so long, and our relationship improved once Janet was able to stop scratching her head and asking me: 'When are you going to grow up?' I'd finally done it. I might have been 47 years old, but I'd flipping well done it! *Loose Women* would love it, I thought, because it had been a running joke on the show for years that I still lived with my mother.

I'm so grateful to Sue. She stuck her neck out by speaking up, and it paid huge dividends. Henrik hadn't wanted to share the house with my mother but I'd talked him into it, and who knows what toll that took on our marriage? I'll never know the answer to that question but, thanks to Sue, I learned a vital life lesson from the failure of my marriage to Henrik. It wasn't just that I needed to know when to cut the apron strings with my mum. Sue had shown me that sometimes you need to have difficult conversations, and that you mustn't be afraid to have them.

As Ed's retirement loomed in 2010, I sat him down and we had the biggest talk ever. It was the first time in my life I had talked frankly with a man, adult to adult, about how we both saw the relationship, and what was needed to make it work. In the past I'd been out with men who didn't like the fact I had a big career. It's not the world people of my age were brought up in, and so many men found it intimidating that I was an independent woman, earning the same amount of money as them, or more. I can see now that power struggles spoiled quite a lot of relationships before they got off the ground, and I was determined that once Ed left The Searchers, things didn't go wrong between us. We needed to be clear about what his retirement meant for both of us and how things would change, because I was still working – and working very hard – and we both had to be happy.

I thought it all through, and I took the bull by the horns.

'For this to work,' I said to Ed, 'I need you to take care of our home and make sure everything is done, so that I don't have to do it all when I have time off. That doesn't mean you have to do everything yourself. If there's something you can't do, or don't want to do, get someone in to do it. That way, when I'm back we can sit on the sofa, chill out and spend time together.'

Ed was totally on board. He'd never had a conventional home life and was looking forward to having a rest, pottering around the garden and doing whatever men do in their sheds. As soon as my mother moved out he took over all the cooking, which he was brilliant at, and he bought some cameras and took up photography. 'Is that going to be enough to keep him happy?' I thought, but Ed was in heaven. 'Bored yet?' I'd say, and his reply was either 'No, loads to do' or 'Not yet, but I'd like to be bored, I've never had the chance before!'

It didn't matter how much time I spent working away, either on tours or, later on, when I started making my cruising and holiday shows, Ed was very happy to stay at home.

Even when I went to Australia for weeks on end, he stayed behind in Wakefield. 'Are you sure you don't want to come?' I said. 'No, when I was touring I always spent six weeks in Australia,' he replied. 'I've done it so many times, and anyway it's work for you. You'll be back.'

'Don't you get fed up of seeing me like this?' I said to Ed one day. I know some people like to imagine I live in sequins and swan around in fluffy mules, sipping champagne, but of course it's not like that at all, and never has been. As usual, I was in comfy pants and a baggy sweater, wearing no make-up and dunking a biscuit in a mug of tea.

'No, I prefer you like this,' Ed said. 'You're my Jane, nobody else sees you like this.'

That was the right answer, bless him!

As well as taking care of the home, Ed supported me in my career. We talked at length about the business, and all the failures of the past. 'If we're gonna do this, let's do it properly,' Ed said, and he was with me every step of the way when I teamed up with Martin and began to learn the business from top to bottom, upping my game on stage and underwriting my own tours. I surrounded myself with the best people I could afford, and that's a tip I'd give anyone, whether you are in the entertainment industry or not. Having great people around you should never be seen as a threat; it's the opposite, because it spurs you on, helps you to keep improving and safeguards you against failure.

Ed also taught me how to manage my personal finances, sorting out everything from my mortgage to savings and investments. It wasn't rocket science. Ed was like my dad, giving safe, sound advice, like putting money away for a rainy day and getting rid of debts and interest charges I didn't need to be paying.

My years with Ed were fabulous and I will never be able to thank Sue enough for intervening the way she did. It takes courage to stick your head above the parapet, but when the stakes are high and you care about the people involved you just have to do it. I had so many failed relationships before Ed, but maybe that's what I had to do, so it eventually worked out for us. When things go wrong, in any aspect of your life, you have to trust in the future and know that things *will* get better. Without all the boyfriends and break-ups over the years, including the failure of my marriage to Henrik, and the mistake that was bringing Jarek to work with me, I'd have been a different person when I met Ed again in my forties, and we would not have had the wonderful 13 years we spent together.

TRUSTING YOUR GUT

'Don't be afraid of change'

'Tomorrow you'll be swimming with sharks, Jane.'

'You what? Are you joking?'

Nope. This wasn't a joke. It was 2016 and I was in the Bahamas, making my first ever episode of *Cruising with Jane McDonald*. As I've said, when I signed up for *Cruising* I had a few worries about whether I'd pull off being a travel presenter. It was new territory to me, but I went for it because of my reaction to Channel 5's super talented Ben Frow, and having a good feeling about us working together. I didn't really have a clue what I was letting myself in for, but I trusted my instincts and that's what made me take the plunge.

Now I was *literally* taking the plunge, diving into a sea of sharks while carrying a load of shark bait. *What on earth?* I felt nauseous with nerves as I went over the side of the dive boat but I went for it all the same, reminding myself that I was in safe hands, with an expert diving team and my experienced film crew all looking out for me. Once I saw the sharks swimming serenely around me my nerves started to melt away and I began to appreciate what an absolute privilege it was to be in this underwater wonderland. It was absolutely *magical*.

We make so many excuses in life for not taking risks, especially as we get older, but that dive made me determined to make the most of all the opportunities *Cruising* would bring. If you always stay in the shallows, you don't get to experience the world beyond your comfort zone, and as the sharks reminded me, what an incredible world it is.

That said, my mother always taught me that there's a big difference between going out of your comfort zone and knowing when to walk away. 'Don't get the two confused,' she said. 'To go out of your comfort zone is good for you, but if your gut is telling you this feels wrong, then you shouldn't be doing it, and you need to walk away.' I reminded myself of that when I stepped up to sing the song at the end of my first episode of *Cruising*. Ben was convinced it was a brilliant idea, but I was still having the collywobbles about it, right up to the wire. 'Will I just look daft? Will people think it's corny?' This was uncharted water, and I really had no idea whether the song would sink or swim.

It felt just like being 15 again, auditioning for a part in the Thornes House Secondary School production of *The Wizard of Oz*. Despite all the singing lessons I'd had, this could go wrong; I might not be good enough, even for a place in the back of the chorus. Not to mention the fact the bullies would love it if I failed. Part of me wanted to turn on my heel and not put myself through it, but of course I didn't do that. I wanted to at least try, and what was the worst that could happen?

'Can I sing this song?' I said quietly to the music teacher, Brian Murrison. I had chosen 'The New Moon', a classical song for a soprano voice, because it was one I'd been practising with my singing teacher, Len Goodwin. Mr Murrison looked at me in surprise. I think he'd been expecting me to go for 'Over the Rainbow', which would have been the safer and more obvious option, but I felt this song was just perfect for the audition.

Nobody was more surprised than me when Mr Murrison gave me the leading role, his jaw having hit the floor after hearing me sing. Playing Dorothy gave me a huge shot of self-confidence, one I desperately needed in my teenage years. I'd taken a chance and it paid off, and when I stood on that school stage, hearing the applause from the audience at the end of the show, I knew I was on my way: for the first time ever I really believed I could make it as a performer, and that was such a huge moment in my life.

Fast-forward 38 years, and there I was again, risking it for a biscuit and singing my heart out in front of a brand new, untested audience. Once again, there was no guarantee this would work out for me, but my instincts were telling me to just give it my best shot and see what happened next. Happily the closing song did go down well – very well, in fact. It became a real draw for *Cruising* viewers, and it was fabulous to have a string to our bow that no other travel show had. Every week viewers would take to social media trying to guess what I was going to sing on a windswept Scottish island or while I was sailing down the Danube, and I really looked forward to it too. I have some great, fun memories of recording those songs, and one of the best was when I went to Barbados, for the seventh series.

'Thank you, Barbados, for an unforgettable trip of a life-time,' I said, after drinking delicious coconut milk, fresh from the shell. 'I can't say goodbye without singing a song which will always remind me of the joy this island gave me – DNCE's "Cake by the Ocean".'

Honest to God, I had no idea what I was singing about, but it was a joy to sing and dance in the glorious Caribbean sunshine. The internet enjoyed my performance too; I found out later that people had a great giggle at my expense, speculating online about just how naive I was, and whether I really thought I was singing about Victoria sponge, rather than sex on the beach!

So many good things came out of presenting *Cruising*. It was fantastic to be back on the open sea – I genuinely do love a cruise – but this time with a totally different focus (not to mention far more luxurious cabins than the ones I was used to when I was working on the ships). I got to visit so many places I never would have seen, and that's *priceless*. One of the highlights for me was the breathtakingly beautiful view of the sea and the hills from Larnach Castle near Dunedin in New Zealand, another was visiting the incredible Fingal's Cave in Scotland. I felt grateful for the opportunities I had every day but, by heck, it was hard work.

I had no idea how tiring making the series would be; we were up at the crack of dawn every day and typically didn't stop filming until around 10pm. I discovered I'm a 'seat of your pants' type of presenter, happier thinking on my feet and reacting in the moment than sticking rigidly to a script. The TV critics said my style of presenting was refreshing, making viewers feel they were right beside me as I sniffed the posh smellies in the bathroom or struck up impromptu conversations with the locals. I loved that, but the GoPro camera stick was the real star of the show. It meant I could go off on my own and explore without a camera crew and it was so unobtrusive it helped put everyone at ease and made the footage as natural as it could be.

Another stroke of genius from the producers was getting me to swim with the sharks in episode one. From that moment on, whenever I thought 'I really can't do this' I would feel the fear and do it anyway. At the end of the day I was in safe hands, and so I said yes to all the challenges that came my way. 'How hard can it be?' I asked myself. 'Come on, you can do it. Think how you'll feel afterwards.'

That's how I came to agree to get in a Perspex tub inside a pool of crocodiles in Australia, signing a death waiver before I did so.

'Always read the small print, because you could die,' I said in my voiceover. Of course there was an element of fear involved, but I lived to tell the tale and it was another risk worth taking, because it was as exhilarating and awe-inspiring as it was frightening. The same goes for jumping 192 metres off the 53rd floor of the Auckland Sky Tower. Once again I put on a brave face and got on with it, trusting my gut when it told me the safety ropes were top notch and I was not going to land with a splat on the pavement. My heart was going like a train, but I did it, and it was another incredible memory to take away.

Sue was always with me on those shows, as my PA as well as my hair and make-up artist, and that was a real godsend. Not just because she stopped me from looking like

I'd been dragged through a hedge backwards after those hair-raising stunts, but it was a comfort to have my best pal with me for a chinwag and some moral support. I really needed that, because I was on a very steep learning curve when I first started on *Cruising*. For instance, there were days when I felt we went over the top with the amount we shot, and I would get cranky when I was asked to do things for a second time. Either I thought the 'retakes' were unnecessary, or I worried that it was my fault because I hadn't got it right first time. In hindsight, I can see that instead of moaning or fretting, what I should have done was ask the crew to explain exactly why they needed me to go again. When I did ask the right questions, the answer always helped. 'We just need a different angle,' they'd say, or 'The light wasn't right.' Everybody makes mistakes when they are learning a new craft, but I could have saved myself some trouble by having a lot more of those conversations early on.

Having Sue there to talk things through with at the end of a long day's filming helped no end. She's a straight talker, is Sue, and sometimes I just needed her to help me see the wood for the trees and tell me I was doing okay. Having that kind of support is so important, to all of us. We all need good teammates around us, because nobody can do it on their own. It doesn't matter how old you are or what expertise or experience you have, when you are learning a new job I would say to anybody that you should listen to your gut feelings and ask yourself: 'What am I worried about? What do I need to know?' Never be afraid to speak up, ask others for help or admit you don't know it all. All of those things are signs of strength, not weakness, and it will help build the best team around you.

My *Cruising* shows got better and better as time went on. The more I found my feet, the more I was myself, completely. I would say whatever came into my head, innuendoes included, because it was what I'd say even if the cameras weren't on me. 'He's the only person with balls this big,' I declared in a spectacular Christmas shop in Switzerland, pointing to a gigantic bauble hanging from the ceiling. It was great to have a laugh and feel free to follow my instincts, saying and doing whatever came naturally to me. I bounced excitedly on the beds in my cabin, I flirted with captains, I dressed up as all sorts, including a cowgirl, and I made covers of everything from 'Club Tropicana' to 'Mambo Italiano', which saw me dancing through the streets of Naples. Some of my best bits were often the 'outtakes' that didn't get taken out, or impromptu moments when I raised a cheeky eyebrow at the men in tight trunks on the beach. I loved all that.

'I've got the best job in the world!' I said every week, as I larked around in my swimming cossie or sipped a fruity cocktail with my fellow passengers. 'This is fabulous! Just fabulous!' I didn't care what I looked like, or if I made a fool of myself. Nor did the producers; in fact they encouraged me to just be me. It was the polar opposite to what happened to me after *The Cruise*, when the 'star makers' tried to airbrush who I really was. Back then I was told to cover up more, because I was 'too old' for bare arms, or I was asked to knock the edges off my accent, because I sounded 'too common'. There was none of that now. I was allowed to be myself, warts an' all, and what a liberating gift that was.

The audience figures for *Cruising* rose to an average of more than 2 million views per episode, and it became the biggest show on Channel 5. Not only that, cruise holiday sales shot up, as did the sale of all the clothes and accessories in my holiday wardrobe. Who'd have thought it? I was bowled over by the success of the show, and then it went to another level again, when we were nominated for a BAFTA in 2018. Seriously, who'd have seen *that* coming?

When I got the call from Channel 5, inviting me to the ceremony at the Royal Festival Hall in February, I was in Wakefield, up to my eyeballs in work.

'I can't go,' I said, thinking it was impossible to go to London and back.

'You've got to! Please come!'

'I can't,' I said. 'I'm too busy working, doing your show!'

Of course I had to be there, busy schedule or not. Sue picked my frock, a fantastic rose-gold Jacques Azagury number, and Ed came with me, looking gorgeous in a tuxedo. I'm not one for showbiz events and rarely go to those kind of dos, and this was the first time Ed and me had been to anything like this together. I think some folk thought I'd made him up before he walked me up the red carpet that night, and I was so proud to have him on my arm.

I didn't think for a moment that we'd win the BAFTA and I had refused to write a speech 'just in case', because what was the point?

'Let's just enjoy the nomination,' I said. 'That's enough,'

I was *flabbergasted* when *Cruising with Jane McDonald* was announced as the winner in the Features category. Mark Powell, my fabulous executive producer, had had the good sense to prepare a speech for me and, in typical style, when I read it out I confessed to the audience that it was his work, and he had even written 'wow!' as the start. That got a laugh, and the laughter kept coming all night – or at least until I reluctantly had to leave the dinner and after party early, to get to Salford for a recording the next morning. Still, I was absolutely elated, and I was walking on air for days and weeks afterwards. The cherry on the cake was that this was Channel 5's first ever BAFTA. What an incredible achievement for everybody involved – and how glad was I that I took the plunge and said yes to Ben Frow!

On the back of my success with *Cruising*, Ben asked if I fancied doing another programme for Channel 5.

'What else would you like to do?' he asked.

Blimey, what a compliment that was, and what an opportunity. I gave it some thought. I now had my dream team with me when I went on tour, with Martin at the helm as tour manager. And as well as my fabulous band, we had two fantastic backing singers, Gina McKendrick and Sarah Rhodes, who also danced and looked amazing. Our staging was top notch too. I wanted the audience to enjoy a night of brilliant entertainment and to go home with a song in their heart, thinking, 'That were flipping fabulous!' – and that's what we achieved, night after night as we toured the country.

Starring as Grizabella in *Cats* back in 2015 had given me a lot of confidence in my voice, which helped take my performance on tour to another level. The vocal coach on *Cats* had told me: 'You have no idea how big your voice is', which gave me such a boost, and the training I was given every day really stretched me. It meant that when I was back on the road with my own shows I felt I could sing *anything,* and I did, taking on ambitious numbers like 'The Greatest Showman'. I also sang 'Memory' every night too (enjoying being dressed in sequins and bling, rather than as an ageing cat) and it went down a storm. 'Wow, she's changed!' people said. 'I didn't know she could do that!' I not only had *Cats* to thank for upping my game, but by this time Seán Barry was on board as our MD. Seán had been recommended to me by Steve, who by then had been the guitarist in my band for years, and from day one it felt like Seán was the missing piece of the puzzle we didn't know we needed. With Martin steering the ship, we took *Jane & Friends* all over the country, and it became the biggest selling show in theatre at the time.

The banter I had with the audience was an integral part of the show's success, and the fact I now felt comfortable with everyone I worked with really set me free on stage. It took me back to some of my favourite nights in the working men's clubs when I was in my early twenties, winning awards like Best Club Singer. The atmosphere was electric, and I was buzzing every night when we got back on the tour bus after another cracking show.

'Come and see me on tour,' I said to Ben Frow, in answer to his question. 'I'd like to do what I do in theatres, on telly.'

And that's exactly how my Channel 5 TV show *Jane & Friends* came about. Except it wasn't just what I did on stage, we had star guests too, like Bonnie Tyler, Tony Hadley, Elkie Brooks and Billy Ocean, plus features like 'Jane's Heroes' celebrating unsung members of the public who did very special things. There was dancing too, and prizes, and the interaction with the audience was fabulous. My band became my TV house band, and we brought in Ami Evans as a third backing singer alongside Gina and Sarah. The girls were in a very successful trio called The Bluebirds, and having all three on board worked so well that Ami ended up joining us on tour as well as on TV. It felt like everything had clicked into place. *Jane & Friends* was a fabulous, primetime variety show, something I'd always dreamed of hosting.

Life was hectic, to say the least. As well as making *Jane & Friends* and *Cruising,* I had started presenting other travel shows, like *Holidaying with Jane McDonald* and *Jane McDonald's Weekends Away.* On top of that I was touring every year, putting on a minimum of 36 dates around the UK, mostly across the summer months. I was booked solid and that's a fantastic position to be in – 'three jobs Jane' had the three best jobs in the world. I'd like to say that I was living the dream, and in many ways I was. *Jane & Friends* was the perfect show for me and I have great memories of it, my all-time favourite being when Ed came on with a snare drum and drummed for us in our New Year's Eve special at the end of 2018. It was beautiful. I was in heaven that night and we had so much fun, but making the show brought its challenges too.

We recorded *Jane & Friends* in front of a live audience, making three fabulous series from 2017 onwards. I thrived on having the live audience to bounce off, but filming always felt like such a rush. I was running on adrenaline, always arriving at the studio wishing I had more time. I should have been relishing every moment – this was everything I wanted, from when I was a little girl watching Bruce Forsyth and Cilla on Saturday night TV – but in hindsight I was simply too busy to make the most of it, and that was frustrating. We also had some issues with our transmission dates that I had no control over, which contributed to the feeling that every-thing was being done in a hurry. I wasn't just flying by the seat of my pants, I was doing it at a million miles an hour.

One day, in 2019, I made a bold decision.

'This is the last one I'm doing,' I announced.

I was the executive producer, and that was it, my word was final. It was a risky decision, because what if I never got the chance to do another primetime show? I did worry about that, but ultimately I followed my instincts and did what my body was telling me to do. That day was the worst of my TV career, but I knew I had to walk away. I was spreading myself too thin, something had to give and unfortunately for *Jane & Friends*, my gut decided that was it.

The following year I decided to step down from *Cruising* too, after filming the last show in my USA series in February 2020. The reason was simple – after going on 45 cruises in the four years I had been making the show, I desperately needed a break. 'There's only so many beds you can jump on and go "ooh!"' I joked, but the reality was that I was so tired out I felt in danger of burning out. Unfortunately, the schedulers couldn't interrupt filming to give me the time off I needed, because it's all or nothing with a successful series like that. I understood completely, and that's how I ended up handing the baton to Susan Calman, who ran with it brilliantly, and is still doing a fabulous job today.

People were surprised that I hung up my deck shoes when the show was doing so well, but I'd had a ball cruising the world and we'd won the BAFTA, and I like to go out on a high. It felt like exactly the right decision, and when I feel so sure inside, it's never a difficult call to make. Besides, I'm a firm believer that whenever you step away from something you are creating space and gaps so that other things can come in, and there is *always* something waiting for you. Look at what happened when I left the *Century*, disgruntled at never being the headline act. I sensed I had to take that risk in order to progress, and 'boom' – my career took off. To be a success in life you *must* take risks, and it follows that you also have to be prepared to fail. I've never stopped believing that, and I've learned to trust that if you do make a bad decision, it won't be the end of the world because the next opportunity will be along soon to fill the gap the failure has left behind. Juggling more than one job has always helped me keep the faith in this belief: if you don't have all your eggs in one basket, you can afford to take a risk and drop one, and that's a great driver of success.

Despite stepping back from *Cruising* I carried on presenting *Holidaying with Jane McDonald*. It was always a brilliant show to make, and having more space around it in my diary made me appreciate all the more how lucky I was to have this opportunity. When I was younger I used to return to the same tried and tested holiday resorts over and over again. The Canaries was a go-to place when I worked in the clubs. Every January and February the islands would fill up with artists from the clubs, all taking a break after the Christmas season and loving the fabulous tan they got there, thanks to the wonderful warm winds blowing in off the Atlantic. I'd happily plant myself on a sunbed with a book and a piña colada and stay there for a week, not venturing outside the resort. I can't believe I did that now. There's a whole world out there, so why not go and experience it?

I never had a say in any of my destinations for *Holidaying*, and it was always exciting finding out what was in store. I screamed when I was told we were off to the American South, and what a fabulous trip that was. Just to spend a night in New Orleans was a dream come true; the whole place was so alive with music, I was in my element. We sailed along the Mississippi on the world's largest steamboat and we also travelled to Memphis to visit Graceland. 'Elvis's house!' I gasped. 'We're here! Oh wow!' I was in paradise; that trip was everything I imagined and more.

I wasn't quite so keen when I was told I was going on safari in Kenya in 2022. I don't know why safaris had never really appealed to me and I wasn't sure I'd enjoy it, but of course I kept that to myself. I was incredibly fortunate to have this chance, and I'd make the most of it, come what may. Oh my goodness, when I look back now, what on earth was I thinking? We stayed in a remote tented camp in Laikipia, and spending the night under the stars was the most magical experience of my life; I didn't want to close my eyes because the stars were just so mesmerising. Every day I'd wake up buzzing, excited about what the day would bring. We saw elephants, giraffes and zebra up close and, most memorably of all, we saw a lioness interacting with her cubs, just a few metres in front of us. It's an image I'll take to my grave, I really will. It moved me to tears, and I will never forget it. It's the best trip I've ever, ever done, and Sue agrees.

Funnily enough, the last *Holidaying* shows I made were all about the Canaries, before I stepped down from making that series too, in 2023. Perhaps I'd come full circle? It felt like that, in a way. I'd been all over the world and had the most incredible experiences, and once again my gut was starting to tell me it was time to make space for other challenges and opportunities. As always, I wanted to leave the party while I was still having fun. I had a winning team around me on *Holidaying* and we were having the best time ever, which I think always translates to the screen. In March 2022, 4.4 million watched my four-part Caribbean special, and cruise bookings with Sovereign Holidays shot up by 75 per cent. *The Times* ran a piece on me under the headline 'Jane McDonald – the world's least likely travel influencer', the article stating: 'The former cruise-ship singer is bookings gold – move over Kim Kardashian!' Honestly, how crazy is that? The *Guardian* also gave me the thumbs up, after a fashion. '*Jane McDonald: Lost in Japan* – she's no Anthony Bourdain,' their headlined read, 'but watching her is aston-ishingly joyous.' I'll take that!

Wanting to slow down a bit, and have more time for myself and my music, also played a part in my decision to step back from *Holidaying*. I'm not getting any younger – I turned 60 in April 2023 – and the filming schedule could be very demanding. On the cruises we were always constrained by the ship's schedule, and that meant we had to hit a lot of filming deadlines before we sailed off to the next port. On *Holidaying*, I'd imagined we could work at a more leisurely pace, given we had the luxury of visiting one holiday loca-tion at a time, on our own timetable. But I was wrong about that. We still had regular 5am starts and 10pm finishes, and when I got back from each trip, let's just say I certainly didn't feel like I'd been on holiday!

What finally clinched it for me was when I stopped doing my song at the end, a decision that was out of my hands. The viewers still adored the song, but new programme makers came in with different ideas about how to spend the production budget. I understand you can't always do every-thing you want to do, but for me the show didn't feel the same without the closing song. It was so popular with the viewers, and as soon as I heard it was going it made up my mind: it was time to go. It was a decision I made very easily, all things considered. You know it's right when you don't have to agonise over something. And I didn't look back, not once. I only ever look forward. That said, if I'm very honest I don't think that part of my life is over just yet. I believe there are more travel adventures to come and more programmes to make, but who knows what's around the corner?

When people asked me 'what's next?' I took great pleasure in saying, 'I've got no idea, but I know there's something else for me out there.' One thing I was adamant about was that whatever the next thing was, if it didn't make me go 'hell yeah!' I wouldn't do it. That's my acid test nowadays.

✳ ✳ ✳

'Jane, Live Nation want to do your next tour.'

'Live Nation?' I repeated back to Martin Hudson. 'Did you just say Live Nation? As in "the biggest promoter in the world Live Nation"?'

'I did, Jane, yes.'

'Hell yeah! Bring it on!'

It was 2023 and, after years of successful tours, and doing it all ourselves, this would be quite a move. I'd be giving back a lot of the jobs I'd taken over myself, such as selling tickets and basically running the company from our tour bus, but I had no qualms about doing that, not with Live Nation. I would still be keeping an eye on everything – I'd never blindly hand over to control to anyone, ever again – but I wouldn't have to be overseeing all the admin side of things myself, in-house. Live Nation, and their agents Cuffe and Taylor, would do all that so I could focus on my set, choosing my stage outfits and delivering a fantastic concert, which is what it's all about. It was a fabulous endorsement for how far we'd come and Martin and I were cock-a-hoop.

I know this sounds a bit daft, but I feel like there's much more ahead for us. I can see us in arenas. I don't know if you feel the same.

More than a dozen years had passed since I said that to Martin, and since he had replied, 'Yes, I do. When you're ready, let's work on it.' Of course, I'd done my Christmas concert at Leeds Arena in 2018, but this would be a complete theatre and arena tour of more than 20 venues, kicking off at the Blackpool Opera House in October 2024. It was everything I'd not only been dreaming of but manifesting for a very long time. As I write, some of the concerts in my *With All My Love* tour have already sold out, and more dates have been added. I couldn't be more thrilled and excited.

* * *

I'm a big believer in manifesting your goals. When you know in your gut what you want to make happen, and you visualise your dreams coming true, I'm convinced it helps turn them into reality. And when your instincts are strong, hell or high water are not going to stop you chasing your goals and willing them into existence. There have been lots of times in my life when I've practised this. When I was in my thirties I did it with a car, would you believe? I didn't really believe it myself at the time, but it's totally true. I went to a Jaguar garage and saw all these fantastic cars, but they were silly money and there was no way I could afford one. 'Right, I'm gonna try manifesting this,' I thought. I kept picturing one of the cars on my driveway and I was really *feeling* it, as if it were actually there, parked outside the house. And then guess what happened? I got a phone call from the garage, saying someone had paid a huge deposit and then pulled out, and would I like to take over the purchase, at 60 per cent of the full asking price? I didn't hesitate; I was so sure this was meant to be.

I always have a bit of manifesting on the go, and right now I'm dreaming of having a house by the sea. I've always been drawn to the sea, ever since I was a little girl and we went to the beaches at Bridlington, Scarborough and Filey – the east coast was as far as Dad's old van could get! Mum once told me that the very first time I saw the sea as a small child my face lit up and I gave it a round of applause. 'You squealed with delight and clapped and clapped,' Mum said. 'People were stopping and looking at you, because you were so enraptured.' Just thinking about our old family holidays brings back the smell of the sea, the sound of the seagulls squawking and the feeling of the wind blowing through my hair. It would be bliss to have a bolthole by the sea, where I could spend my downtime, look out of the window and give the sea a clap whenever I wanted to. I know that's a dream for so many people, and who knows if it will happen for me? Maybe I'll just rent a little place for a while, but let's see. Even if your dream doesn't come true in exactly the way you want it to, I think manifestation is a positive force that helps you move forward in the direction you want to go.

Manifesting success as a performer has helped me no end. It's essentially what I do when I feel nervous backstage and I make myself think about how fabulous I will feel when the show is in full swing and everyone is having the best time ever. I get as much joy from a show as the audience, if not more, and I remind myself of that, and of how unbelievable that feeling is. Envisaging the whole show unfolding, and feeling it happening, really gives me the confidence that it *will* all be as fabulous as I hope.

On a larger scale, I manifested playing arenas after I started to tour again a few years on from Henrik, when mine was not the hottest ticket in town and I couldn't even sell out a theatre. 'Yes, I'll get there,' I told myself. 'Yes, I'll do arenas one day. I *know* I will. This is absolutely going to happen.' I saw myself on the stage of a big arena, and once I'd done Leeds Arena I kept on manifesting a whole arena tour. Talking to Martin about it was all part of turning the dream into a reality, and keeping the faith that it would happen one day gave me the courage to start underwriting my own shows and tours.

'I don't know how you sleep at night,' Sue said, when I first put up my house as collateral, many years ago. Of course it was a risk, but to me it was a calculated and necessary risk, because it would help me realise my dreams, and they were absolutely coming true. 'You have to jump of a cliff to see if you can fly,' I've said many times, or in the words of Kurt Vonnegut: 'We have to continually be jumping off cliffs and developing our wings on the way down'.

We've taken a big leap with Live Nation, but I'm thrilled we have and I know it's going to work out. You have to keep evolving in order to grow your wings, and on this tour there will be more focus on me as an artist. A lot of people still think I just do covers and I want to show that I write my own material and play the piano too. It's a new brave direction for me on stage, but one that feels so right. Every day I keep picturing a sold-out tour and I'm doing all I can to make that happen, manifesting 'sold out' signs at theatres and envisaging all the joyous faces in the audience, and people saying it's been the best show I've ever put on. I can't wait.

* * *

'Would you like to do *Celebrity Gogglebox*?' my agent asked.

'Would I?' I thought, taking a moment as I considered my reaction. I love watching the show and find it hilarious, but then again, did I really wanted to be *in* it, and have cameras on me when I was sat there with a glass of wine, watching TV?

My gut has been telling me for years what I should and shouldn't be doing, and at last I've mastered the art of properly listening to my body, not just when it suits me, but every time it's talking to me. I've learned the hard way, mind you. Years ago, I was about to sign a contract when I noticed that one important thing I asked for was missing. When I queried it I was told, 'Don't worry, it'll go in, Jane.' I wasn't convinced, and I should have listened to my gut, because that clause never did go in and I was not a happy bunny. When it comes to men, I've not listened to my gut more times than I care to remember. I got it right occasionally when I was younger – I instinctively knew I had to let Ed go the first time round, and I listened to that – but there have been plenty of other times when my solar plexus has been screaming at me, 'Will you just listen?' and I've ignored it and gone, 'It'll be fine. I'll just do it this one time, and then we'll see.' I don't make those mistakes anymore. When my gut is talking to me, I sit up straight and listen, because as Mum told me, if it feels right, it's right, and if it feels wrong, it's wrong.

We all get choices to make every day, and it's up to us to test out our reaction and decide what to do. I wasn't worried at all about the nuts and bolts of making *Celebrity Gogglebox*. Like I say, I'm a 'seat of your pants' girl, and being unscripted and recording 'as live' suits me down to the ground – what you see is what you get, and there is only one version of me. So, what was making me hold off on an immediate 'hell yeah'? I think that when you are in a comfortable, safe place, feeling content in your world, it's easy to want to stay there and avoid making any changes. I've struggled so much in my life and it's so tempting to stop pushing myself, because I don't feel the need to do that anymore, at least not in terms of building my profile or career. But change for me is growth, and I've grown from every change I've ever made in my life, so actually I still need to push myself out of my comfort zone. We all do.

'I'll do it if my best mate can do it with me,' I said, probably sounding like I was back at Thornes House Secondary School.

'Hell yeah!' the *Gogglebox* producers said, or words to that effect, and then I was really up for it too, and excited at the opportunity.

Sue is the biggest fan of *Gogglebox* and watches it all the time. I remembered she once said that she'd love to go on it, and I'd never heard her say anything like that before. I knew she'd be brilliant on the show too, because as well as always saying what she sees, Sue has a really dry, quick sense of humour.

We recorded the show in 2023 and had such a laugh doing it. I mean, what's not to like about sitting on the sofa with your best mate, a giant glass of wine in your hand (yes, the viewers did comment on the size of our glasses!) while you eat crisps non-stop and watch all the best bits of telly? Sue and I make a good double act, I think; when I'm in fairyland she's the realist who brings me down to earth with one quip, usually with perfect comic timing. It was great for Sue to get some recognition and viewers loved her, as I knew they would. At the end of the day we are just two women of a certain age who have a funny bone and like a laugh. We're no threat to anybody, and if you don't like us, it won't bother us. It's great when you get to that stage in your life, when you don't really care what people think of you. When the cameras started rolling it took Sue and me all of two minutes to forget about the outside broadcast crew parked up outside the house. 'God help us,' I said, after our first recording. 'We'll either be arrested or we'll never work again!' I'm happy to say neither happened, and *Celebrity Gogglebox* invited us back, which is fabulous.

Who knows if this opportunity, like so many others, would have come along if I'd not grasped all the chances that came before it? As I always say, I believe everything happens for a reason. To reach this point I've done my best to listen to my gut, to know when to take a leap of faith or when to walk away. And I'm proud to say I've embraced so many challenges, even when it meant going way out of my comfort zone, swimming with sharks or jumping off buildings. Some experiences have been better than others, but that's life. I'm glad I took on each and every opportunity, because life is for living, and even if you change your mind, tire yourself out or wish things had gone differently, at least you've given it a shot and have a new story to tell.

Right then, Sue, pass us them crisps, the programme's starting . . .

GROWING THROUGH GRIEF

'You don't move on, you move forward'

'Let's take it nice and slow,' Ed said. 'It's not a race.'

It was the summer of 2020 and the two of us were walking round Newmillerdam, a beautiful country park a few miles from home. It's one of those places that always lifts my spirits, and I was counting my blessings. Ed and I had really made the most of the lockdown, enjoying spending more time together than ever before. Pottering around doing ordinary things, like gardening and watching boxsets, was so lovely that my decision to retire had been easy. Ed was right; it was time to slow down, and that's what I was going to do, at last.

Ed and I were on a level now, and that felt great. When we first met he was the big, crazy, fun-loving rock-and-roll star. He was beautiful too. Though Ed had changed in so many ways – home was the only place he wanted to be now, surrounded by peace and tranquility – he was still a beautiful man, inside and out. I felt so lucky to have known the two sides of Ed; I loved them both.

Before I retired I had one last TV job to do, filming on a luxury barge on the River Thames. This was to fulfill the final part of my *Cruising* contract, postponed because of lockdown, and as soon as the restrictions allowed I went down to London to make the programme. I was in a great mood when I called Ed to tell him filming had gone well.

'That's that done!' I said, feeling quite giddy at being one step closer to retirement. 'How are you?'

'I've got this bloody cough I can't shake,' Ed said. 'It's like a bad cold.'

My mind raced back to how Ed had said 'let's take it nice and slow' when we walked in the country park together, a few weeks earlier. Even though he was usually off like a bullet on our walks I'd not thought twice about him walking slowly. Now I thought, *flipping heck, I hope he hasn't got Covid*, though this seemed very unlikely, I reasoned. Ed had been delighted to be forced to stay at home and we were both very strict at following all the guidelines. The conversion of our bungalow into a house had continued, but only because the builders were working at a safe distance, on the opposite side of the property to where we were living. Even when we had skips delivered onto the driveway as we cleared out the attic, Ed and I wore masks and were very careful to keep to the rules. I couldn't think of a single risk we'd taken.

Travelling back to Wakefield, I told myself not to worry. It was probably just a bad cold, as Ed said. He'd be better soon, and at least I was on my way home, to take care of him.

As soon as I walked in the front door, I knew it was more than a cold. Ed looked terrible.

'I can't breathe,' he rasped.

My heart thumped. 'I'm calling the doctor.'

'No,' Ed said, 'please don't. They might send me to the hospital where all the Covid is.'

He meant Pinderfields, the acute District General Hospital in Wakefield. At that time, the news was full of terrible stories about the devastating number of people dying from Covid in hospitals all over the country. I understood Ed's fears, but he was clearly very unwell, and he admitted he hadn't been right for days. 'Darling,' I said, 'you can't go on like this. Let me try to get somebody to the house.'

Ed agreed, and eventually I got a GP to come out and do a home visit. The doctor listened to Ed's chest, looked at me and immediately said: 'I don't like what I'm hearing.' I expected him to send Ed straight to Pinderfields, but the doctor didn't think it was a good idea. 'He's better off at home,' he told me.

Ed was relieved about this, but I wasn't reassured in any way. The doctor offered no other advice or medication, and we were on our own, back to square one. I called another doctor out a few days later, and he said we should go to hospital. *Thank God for that*, I thought, but then the first doctor was consulted again and he disagreed. 'I don't want to send him anywhere,' he said, 'because if he gets Covid . . .' I can't remember if the doctor finished his sentence, but I instinctively sensed what came next: *It could be curtains*.

I couldn't stand by any longer doing nothing, so in desperation I took Ed into Dewsbury and District Hospital, a place he was less wary of. My memories start to fog over at this point, but what I do know is that they took him straight over to Pinderfields, and at the same time they sat me down and said: 'This isn't good news, I'm afraid.'

Wendy works at the hospital, so I rang her to ask if she could tell me anything. Of course she couldn't, and I had to wait to hear the news from a doctor. The diagnosis could not have been worse: Ed had Stage 4 lung cancer and there was nothing they could do.

'You're gonna have to be strong, Jane.' I was in a daze and it felt like everyone was saying that to me, but what do you do? *I can't*, I thought. *He's the strong one. Ed's the strong one, not me.*

They managed to drain his lungs, which thankfully made his breathing easier for a short while, but unfortunately Ed then had a lot of complications caused by the drain and rapidly went from bad to worse. It was as if the moment he heard the diagnosis and knew he wasn't going to survive he started going downhill, fast. I'm so grateful to all the staff at the hospital because they understood Ed was scared to be there. Given there was nothing that could be done to treat him, and that pain management was now all that was on offer, they supported me in taking him home to care for him myself. The district nurse would come out once a week, but other than that, I was on my own. I was taught to do everything the nurses would have done in hospital, like changing dressings and administering drugs, but even so it was terrifying driving home with Ed that day. I'd never done anything like this before, but it would be worth it, because Ed would be happier at home, and he would feel safe.

Once we were back in the bungalow I told Ed we should cancel all the building work; we had far more important things to worry about and I was sure he wouldn't want the bother of the noise and the comings and goings outside.

'No, Jane,' he said. 'I want you to carry on with it all. It's our house and we made all these plans. Let's see them through.'

I wasn't sure this was the right thing to do but I respected his wishes, and I'm so glad I did. The builder was a friend, Tony, and though he was working at the opposite end of the house to where I was nursing Ed, I was so grateful he was there. Even having Tony wave to me from the driveway made me feel less isolated, because I was on my own in a way I'd never experienced before. Ed's spirits were so low that he withdrew into himself, and became very reclusive, and though I was with him all the time, I felt lonely. Every day I did my best to have a good chat and a laugh with Ed, like we always used to, or get him to walk into the garden for a breath of fresh air, but he didn't want to do anything. It was like part of him had already gone. I could see the despair and resignation written all over his face – Ed's life was coming to an end, fighting would do no good, so what was the point in carrying on?

We were in that period of lockdown when you had to choose your bubble and stay in it. Sue said she wished she could be in our bubble, but she has family of her own and of course they came first. In any case, Ed didn't want anyone else there, even Sue. That spoke volumes. Ed and Sue got on like a house on fire. One of my favourite photos of Ed is of him and Sue in their dressing gowns at the back door of the bungalow, laughing their heads off. Now they might never see each other again, but Ed resigned himself to that.

Sue was gutted she couldn't be there to support me. It felt like one minute I was ringing her up saying, 'Isn't the weather fab? I'm loving lockdown, is that a terrible thing to say?' and the next I was telling her how scared I was of losing Ed, and asking how I'd live without him.

'I'm sorry you have to do this on your own,' Sue said, 'but I promise you this, Jane, I'll be there for you when Ed is not.'

Wendy was the one who really talked me through it every day; she's always my go-to in a crisis, is Wendy, and she was fantastic, as always. I needed all the support I could get. Ed was given his diagnosis in the November of 2020, and the timing could not have been worse. Cancer services at Pinder-fields were severely disrupted because of Covid, as they were all over the country, and to compound this a lot of staff were on annual leave around the Christmas period, including

Ed's oncologist and another specialist. I remember going mad about this, but Wendy calmed me down and made me see that none of this was anybody's fault. Nobody could work a miracle and everybody was doing their best, in extremely difficult circumstances.

Nursing Ed was the hardest thing I've ever done in my life. I changed his dressings, gave him his mediation and pain relief and did my utmost to make sure he ate and slept and was as comfortable as possible. All the time I was wondering if I was doing things right. I'd try to get some sleep once Ed was sorted and settled, but then I'd listen to his breathing and think something was wrong, so I'd be up again checking on him.

One night Ed started screaming in agony. He was on morphine, and I had got the dose wrong. I was sleep deprived, and that's how the mistake happened, but that didn't salve my guilt. *What have I done? How could I do that to him?* I was in such a panic I was gasping for air when I phoned the hospital, desperate for help and advice. The nurses were brilliant and didn't make any fuss at all. Instead they calmly reassured me, telling me how to gradually up the dose. 'It's okay, you just got it wrong,' they said. 'Don't worry, you can put it right, he'll be fine.' I did get Ed back on track, eventually, but throughout that night he was screaming out in pain every couple of hours. It was horrendous to see the man I loved in so much agony, and however understanding and lovely the nurses were with me, I felt *I* was the one who had caused him all that pain.

* * *

Despite losing both of my parents I had never dealt with anything like this. Dad died in 1993, when I was 30 and dividing my time between working on the ships and coming home to do summer seasons in the holiday parks. I'd just finished working as the compère and headline singer at the huge Maid Marian in Robin Hood Park in Skegness, which was a fantastic gig, and I was looking forward to spending a bit of time at home. Dad would normally have picked me up at the end of the season, but his eyes weren't as good as they used to be and Mum had talked him out of driving in the dark.

'That's okay, Dave can drive me,' I said.

Dave was my boyfriend at the time. On my final day before the season ended I went home to drop my car off and pick up Dad's rusty old van, and I can still see him at the garden gate, ready to wave me off. I asked him how the van was running and he frowned.

'Playing up a bit,' he said.

'Nothing's changed, then,' I said, smiling and rolling my eyes.

Dad laughed, and then he told me he was looking forward to me coming home, and going back on the road with me. A few weeks earlier he'd complimented me on my singing for the first time in years, and now something made me stop and say something I didn't often say. 'I do love you, you know,' I said.

Dad smiled. 'Yes, I know you do.'

Dave and I had a dreadful journey back from Skegness that night. I couldn't believe our bad luck, because an hour into our two-and-a-half-hour journey, something went bang and the old van conked out. It was 2am, we were in pitch dark, in the middle of nowhere, and there wasn't a phone box in sight. I didn't know what we were going to do because Dad was the only one who would know how to fix the van. Even though it was dead as a doornail, I got Dave to try the key in the ignition one more time, and that's when a miracle happened, and the van sprang back into life. We couldn't believe it, and we finally rattled into the lane behind Silcoates Street at 4am, just as the engine blew again and the van gave up the ghost once more.

It was 9am when Mum knocked at my bedroom door.

'Jane,' she said softly, 'I'm really sorry to bother you, but I think your dad has died.'

To this day I can't explain why she said that so apologetically; she was in shock, I suppose, and now I was too, to say the least. I jumped out of bed and ran out of my bedroom, oblivious to the fact I was stark naked. Mum asked me if I would go and check on Dad, to see if she was right. I can remember throwing on a dressing gown and taking Dave across the landing with me, but when we reached Mum and Dad's bedroom door I froze, realising I couldn't do it. Dave agreed to go in, and a few moments later he reappeared, confirming the worst. My mother was right; Dad had passed. The coroner would later estimate that he died at 2am, exactly the time the van broke down somewhere between Skegness and home. Dad was 69 years old and, as well as having smoked heavily all his life, and worked down the pit, we discovered that he had been diagnosed with an enlarged heart in recent years, which he'd kept to himself.

'If only he'd managed to give up smoking,' I said, when the family GP broke this news. I'd been functioning on autopilot so far, making cups of tea and trying to be strong for Mum. Now I felt a huge rush of grief and sorrow. Could Dad's death have been prevented if he'd looked after himself better? The doctor gave me a resigned look. 'Who's to know whether the stress of giving up smoking might have killed him quicker than carrying on?' We'd never know the answer to that; the only certainty was that Dad had gone, and life would never be the same again.

In the aftermath of Dad's death, the whole family fell apart. My brother and sister were completely distraught and went to pieces, and it was all too much for my mother, who was angry as well as grief-stricken. Dad's paperwork was not in order and she was left with so much to sort out, not least because everything in the house suddenly started to fall apart too. First the fire broke down and then all the electrics went bang. We discovered Dad had little pieces of wire running everywhere, and the electrician who came to help told us the house was a deathtrap. Mum was even more enraged when she heard that. 'How could he leave me in this state?' she vented. 'How *could* he?'

I can see now that Mum's anger was a stage of the grieving process, but I didn't understand that then and was taken aback by it. I tried to reason with her, saying Dad didn't know he was going when he did, but nothing calmed her down. She was consumed by rage. Reluctantly, I realised I had no choice but to step in and take care of all the practicalities, including working out what to do with the house. Janet looked around the house in despair, asking Mum what she was going to do now, because the place was falling apart. My sister had a point; as well as the shoddy electrical work, all the furniture was worn, the tiles around the fireplace were chipped and the back door didn't shut properly. When Dad was alive we all accepted his make-do-and-mend approach. If things went wrong he could always fix it, but what now?

Janet thought Mum should move, but our canny mother had done some thinking, and she came up with the idea of me buying the house from her, seeing as I was the only one in the family who didn't have a mortgage and hadn't put down any roots. In return for giving me a good price for Silcoates Street, all Mum asked was that I made sure she always had a roof over her head. I didn't think twice. It was my turn to care for *her* now, and we agreed that as soon as I got my mortgage and bought the house, Mum could put the money from the purchase into doing it up. It was the perfect solution. And as it turned out, this was not only a win in terms of our housing situation; all the responsibilities I took on after Dad's death taught me so much about myself, and what I was capable of.

Dad had faced more adversity in his life than I will ever know. He was in the army and served in World War Two, though he was very tight-lipped about all that. There was a photograph in the house of him in a paratrooper uniform, frowning and looking horribly thin, somewhere really hot, but that was the only evidence we had that he fought in the war. Similarly, he never spoke about the accident he had down the mine when I was seven. When I was much older, I found out that Dad been making his way to the face of the mine when a trolley broke loose and hurtled straight towards him. As the trolley clipped him, he had a split second to jump onto it or be crushed to death. He jumped, thank God, surviving with a shattered ankle and broken ribs.

Dad was so close to being killed that day, but that was not a headline I ever heard. What I remember very clearly is his resilience, and his determination to get back on his feet. He tried working as a crane driver but didn't like it, and that's how he came to take a less dangerous job back in the mine. He also ran a chimney sweeping business on the side, to make up his money. That was my dad all over.

Dad went through so much, and he taught me so much, in his own, unspoken way. In the weeks after his death I sorted out all his paperwork, arranged his funeral, applied for my first mortgage and began the refurbishing of the house. I was surprised at how resilient I was. Dad's make-do-and-mend approach might have left us with faulty electrics, but it had taught me to be a fixer too, or at least have a go at sticking things back together.

If there's a wall in front of you then find a way to either go over it, under it or around it. Don't just walk away.

That attitude to life is one of the gifts my father gave me, and I'm so grateful to him for that. I'd say to anyone, when you face problems in life, never shrink away. Even when the worst thing has happened, and when you really don't think you have it in you, give it your best shot and you will probably be surprised at your strength, resilience and determination.

Just a few months after losing Dad, my mother and I were living in a beautifully decorated home with everything new, including a gas fire, which was our pride and joy after years of lugging coal up from the cellar. We were safe and comfortable, and I was so proud of what we'd achieved. I also got the van mended, which was quite an unnerving experience. 'You can't have driven this,' the mechanic insisted, 'the engine's blown. The bang you heard was the big end going. The engine is completely seized up.'

I discussed this with my mother, telling her that when we broke down, I thought only my dad would be able to fix the engine. Now I convinced myself he must have somehow helped us remotely, as he passed to the other side.

'We broke down at 2am,' I explained. 'Exactly the time he passed.'

Mum gave a little laugh. 'So he came and got you after all,' she said kindly.

I wasn't laughing. However unbelievable my theory, I was very serious. Believing Dad came to my rescue that night was a great comfort to me, and that's the most important thing. When people are bereaved they often look for signs their loved ones are still around, watching over them or sending messages, perhaps from a visiting robin or a white feather falling at their feet. It might be true and it might not be, but if you believe it and it brings you some comfort, there is no harm in that.

After losing my dad I found it very hard going back to work in the clubs. We were a duo on the road and people were used to always seeing us together. It felt like everyone was asking where he was, all the time, and I couldn't deal with it. 'He's not here today,' I'd say sometimes. I just couldn't bring myself to say he had died; it was too upsetting, and too final.

I can see now I was in denial, to some extent. I was trying to carry on as normal, not just at work but at home, where all my energies were going into helping Mum and making things better for her. But grief has to come out somewhere, and it happened one night when I was on stage at the Albion Road club in Rotherham. Midway through a song I felt my throat constrict and my voice lose power before thinning away to a scratchy whisper. I apologised and left the stage, wondering what was wrong with me.

I went to see my GP the next day, who explained that there was nothing wrong with my voice. I was in an emotional state and this was my body's way of responding to the loss of my father. I took time off, staying at home and reading books for days on end. I've always been able to lose myself in a good book, and this time I got more than I bargained for. In one of the novels there was a touching scene between a little girl and her father, and that was it, the floodgates opened. I remembered Dad giving me my first bike, sprayed with gold paint. I pictured him bringing fresh spuds home from his allotment, and I smiled at all my lovely memories of going ballroom dancing with him on a Friday night. *He was the best dad in the world*, I thought, feeling so grateful I had such a close relationship with him, especially during all the years he'd been my roadie. And that's when the enormity of my loss really hit. I started to cry and I couldn't stop.

Once I'd let it all out, my voice began to recover. Not long afterwards, I made a big decision: I would stop doing the clubs and go back to the ships full-time. I couldn't face the clubs anymore without Dad, and so really I was running away. And that's something else I learned about grief. You might start off being strong, when there is a funeral to arrange and other people to support, but that doesn't mean you have to stay strong. When the dust settles, it's okay to let your guard down. It's okay to be vulnerable, and it's okay to allow yourself whatever time and space you need to lick your wounds and build yourself back up.

Mum was in a much better place now, especially as the house was all fixed up, and she was all for it when I told her my plans. 'I want you to go away and travel the world and write me letters, telling me all about the wonderful things you see,' she told me, and that's exactly what I did.

※ ※ ※

When Mum died in 2018 she was in her eighties, and it was a very different story to my dad's passing. Mum had been in old age for a long time, and in poor health since she had a fall in 2015, breaking her spine in three places. I should have been starting work on my first episode of *Cruising*, but Channel 5 were brilliant, giving me the time I needed to help Mum.

It was devastating to see my busy, vibrant mother bent double, requiring 24/7 care. I nursed her for seven months until she was back on her feet in the summer of 2016, and during that time we spent some really special moments together. I'd always go round at teatime and we'd watch *The Chase*. Then I'd cook Mum's dinner, get her tablets sorted for the night and see that she were settled before I went home to Ed, and had my dinner with him. I cherished that time with Mum. She had spent so many years caring for me, and it was a real pleasure to give something back to her, and show her how much I loved her. One of the things I did regularly was to massage Mum's feet and rub her legs with cream, because they would come out in sores.

'Do you know how lovely it is that I can do all this for you now?' I said one day.

Mum couldn't get her head around that, but it was true.

* * *

I was in Australia in 2018, part way through making a four-part series for *Cruising*, when I sensed something was wrong at home. I couldn't get hold of Mum, and when I rang Tony and Wendy, neither picked up. Later that day my sister-in-law phoned me back, explaining that Mum wasn't well, her blood counts were down and she had been taken into hospital. 'Don't panic,' Wendy said, 'they're saying she's coming home soon.' I know my sister-in-law, and I could tell she was being sensitive, trying to give me the most positive news she could. Nobody wanted me to come racing home from Australia if they could help it, but as soon as Mum was given her diagnosis I was on the next plane home, my four-part series suddenly becoming a three-parter.

I cried a lot on the long flight back. *Pancreatic cancer*. It was a very frightening diagnosis and I couldn't take it in at all. As soon as I was back I sat with Mum in Pinderfields Hospital for a week, terrified this was the end but willing it not to be, and for Mum to be allowed to go home. When she was discharged, it was not the news I hoped for. The doctors were letting her go, but only because they could do no more for her. Mum was in a lot of pain by this time, and though I desperately wanted to care for her in her own home I felt she would be better looked after in Wakefield Hospice. It was the best decision. The staff at the hospice were superb, and when I sat with Mum over the coming weeks, instead of worrying about nursing her and making her comfortable, I had the time to talk to her. I think Mum and me said everything we needed to say to each other, including her telling me not to dare cancel my concert at Leeds Arena. I remember I thanked her for being the best mum ever, and Mum told me she didn't know what she'd done to deserve a daughter like me. I burst into tears when she said that. 'Don't be upset,' Mum said, 'it's just my time.'

* * *

Never in a million years did I think I'd be back in Wakefield Hospice a little over two years later, this time sitting next to Ed's bed. He'd got a kidney stone at the start of 2021 and was unable to pass it. The pain was horrific; Ed was in a terrible state. Knowing he was terrified of going into hospital, the hospice kindly took him in for respite care. From there Ed was taken up to Pinderfields as a day patient for the treatment he needed, and once the kidney stone was sorted I was able to take him home again.

From the beginning Ed had been adamant he wouldn't have chemo, if it were offered.

'You're not mad at me, are you?'

'No,' I said, 'I don't blame you.'

We didn't need a discussion. It would not save him, and we silently agreed there was no point in Ed suffering the side effects of chemo only to prolong his agony.

Ed's doctors thought he would live until June, and their prognosis had a bearing on how much morphine he would have, and how much the dosage would be gradually increased. I didn't think Ed was going to last until June. I was convinced he would go sooner, given that he wasn't fighting and didn't want to suffer any more, but I'm not a medic and I had to follow what the experts thought. It was so hard. Ed had completely given up and he just wanted to die. He had accepted his time was up and he was ready to go but, unlike my mother, he wasn't willing to wait patiently for nature to take its course. It was a very conflicting time for me. I wanted Ed's suffering to end, but I didn't want him to go. It's devastating when you can't fix the person you love most in the world, but I could do nothing to save Ed, or to stop his suffering.

Ed had completely fallen apart by the time we returned to the hospice, this time knowing he would not leave. All I could do was hold his hand, try to say the right things and make sure he was as comfortable as could be. One day I started talking to Ed about 'You Still Lead Me', telling him I'd decided to record it on my next album.

'That's about me,' Ed said.

'No, it's about my mother. I wrote it after she passed, remember? It's the sequel to 'The Hand that Leads Me'.'

Ed was adamant. 'No, it's about me,' he repeated.

'Don't do that to me!' I said, shaking my head. It was March 2021, and Ed was close to the end. Now he'd said that, I knew that every time I sang that song I'd think about both him and my mother. How would I cope with that? It's exactly what happened, of course, when I got back on stage, but I don't mind that anymore. As upsetting as it is to be reminded of my loss it brings me comfort too, thinking of how much I loved them both. If it makes me cry, that's a release. You can't hold grief back, or control it in any way. You have to accept it and embrace it as best you can, because it's a process you have to go through, and fighting it will not help you.

Ed was 67 when he died. He was not meant to leave me, not yet and not like that. We had sorted out our life so we could enjoy spending the rest of our days together but instead I was organising his funeral. It was not the cathartic experience it might have been in any way, shape or form. It was one of those awful Covid funerals, with only 15 people allowed to attend. And with lockdown still keeping everybody inside their houses, for a long while afterwards not many people even knew that Ed had passed. I didn't want to tell anybody unless I had to because, as I found out after my dad died, when you say it out loud that's another level of reality, and you don't want to go there. But it had to come out eventually, and one day I was putting out the bins when I bumped into a neighbour from across the road.

'How's things?' she asked brightly.

'Please don't make me talk about it,' I thought.

I had the most awful feeling inside, and when I told her the news it floored her. She had seen the builders coming and going and assumed life was carrying on as normal. 'What?' she said. 'Ed has *died*?'

For days and weeks after that I didn't want to go out of the house again, or see anybody at all. I didn't want to put myself through the ordeal or retelling the news, and I certainly didn't want to see the shock on people's faces as they tried to take it in. I don't blame anybody for how they reacted. It was the most unbelievable turn of events, nobody had seen it coming and the testing circumstances we were all living under made everything ten times harder, for everybody.

I did a lot of crying after Ed died. I was crying for him to begin with, but I think there comes a point when you stop crying for your loved one and you start crying for you. I was trying to process what had happened, sobbing my heart out as I thought about the trauma of nursing Ed, what we'd both lost and what I was going to do with the rest of my life. That's when Sue came in and took over as Wakefield's answer to Wonder Woman. She knew how hard it had been for me. I had been on my own nursing Ed for four months all told, and during that time I barely slept and was in a constant state of high alert. I was emotionally wrung out, and physically exhausted.

'It's been as hard as it could be,' Sue said, and though she didn't say it straight away, she was thinking to herself, *this is beyond normal grief.* Sue could see that I was traumatised by what I'd been through, and she thought it would be a good idea if I talked to a therapist. I listened to Sue and agreed that the experience of not just losing Ed so rapidly, but becoming his nurse, had been intensely distressing, and frightening too. Thanks to Sue I went to see a PTSD specialist, which was so helpful in terms of understanding what I'd been through. Therapy is never a magic bullet, though. Acknowledging my trauma and talking it through was one thing, but I was still weighed down by grief, struggling to leave the house and unable to face the day. When you are grieving, there is nothing as tempting as shutting yourself away. Home becomes your rabbit hole. It's a place where it's lovely and warm and cosy, and you can hide in the dark where nobody can bother you. It's so much easier to stay there than to put your nose out the door, and in the weeks after Ed's passing, that is exactly what I did.

* * *

My tour was happening three months after Ed died, starting with that first gig at the Warner hotel in Cheshire in June.
As I've said, despite the state I was in I was determined to do
it, even though I knew it would be very hard to get up on
stage and perform the way I wanted to. Sue knew there was
no talking me out of it and, as the start of the tour loomed
closer, she suggested I should ask the GP about taking some
antidepressants, to get me going again and help me through
the coming months. Again I listened. When you are feeling
weak, there is always something strong you can do. Listening
to the good friends and loved ones who have your back, and
taking guidance from them, is a sign of strength, not frailty.

I started taking sertraline – an antidepressant that
increases the levels of the mood-enhancing chemical sero-
tonin in the brain – and I also pushed myself out of the rabbit
hole and back into the world, one baby step at a time. I
started going for walks, sometimes to Sandal Castle, which
is a ruined medieval castle not far from home. I love it there,
and it's somewhere I went with Ed, and where we chatted
about the beauty of Yorkshire and all its amazing history. I
felt better the more I walked, and I'd always climb right to
the top, where I could feel the wind blowing through me.
'Please blow this away,' I said one day. Nature is a great
healer, and I believe that when you ask for help, it comes

from somewhere. Once I was breathing fresh air, seeing blue sky and feeling connected to the world in all its glory again, I felt better, or at least well enough to cope with getting back to work.

It was still a big ask to put on a show; after all, this was no longer baby steps but a giant leap into the spotlight. I did it, of course, and I have the wonderful Warner hotel audience to thank for helping me get through the first show when, as I predicted, singing 'You Still Lead Me' made me break down on stage. The antidepressants obviously hadn't fully kicked in yet, because in the very early stages of the tour I still had the ability to cry and feel different emotions. Sertraline is an amazing drug in many ways, and it certainly helped lift me out of the darkest depths of my grief. I was able to get up on stage and sing, at the next gig and the next, but as time went on there was a price to pay for taking the medication. The medication can take up to six weeks to fully kick in, and it also has several side effects. In my case, it didn't just take away my feelings of grief and sorrow, it flattened all my emotions. I didn't feel sadness and I was no longer crying on stage, but I didn't experience the usual joy and euphoria I feel when I perform either. I wasn't feeling *anything*. I was just there, functioning, and that is not a pleasant place to be, let me tell you.

Chapter Seven

If I'm honest, when I look back over that tour I can barely remember it. Instead of saying, 'I hope she turns up' when I looked in the mirror, I started looking at my reflection and thinking, 'Who the hell are you?' The woman on stage was a stranger to me, an imposter in a Jane McDonald frock, but I did my best every night and completed the tour over the next few months. The concerts went down really well, or so I'm told, and that is a blessing. I would have been so upset if the audience saw the stranger I felt inside.

My next big challenge was a trip to Rhodes, in May 2022. This was another commitment that was in the diary long before Ed died, and one I was adamant I was going to fulfill. It was a very special event, designed for my fans to have a lovely holiday on a Greek island as well as to see me perform. It had sounded so fabulous when we planned it, and I'd been looking forward to it since long before lockdown. When I arrived in Rhodes, I should have been in my element, surrounded by love and beautiful people in a fabulous spa hotel in the sun, but I wasn't. I was still emotionally flatlining because of the antidepressants I was taking, and I felt next to nothing. Emotionally, it's a place I never want to be in again. Just like on the tour, I did my best to keep the show on the road and I know the fans enjoyed themselves, but all my memories of that trip are fogged, and I can hardly remember being there. That's such a shame, and it's something I hope to make up for by arranging another holiday with my fans, one I can embrace and cherish every moment of.

* * *

I've learned that there is no rulebook when it comes to grief. The only certainty is that when you lose someone, you are left with an unwelcome companion called grief. There is no time limit on grieving, and how you deal with it is personal to you, and to the person you have lost. I grieved differently for my parents to the way I grieved for Ed – and still grieve for them all – and that's okay. When you lose a parent, even if they go in a sudden and unexpected way like my dad, it's still the natural order of things. Our parents are meant to go before us and, as hard as it was losing Dad and then Mum, it was not the same as losing Ed. My future was not tied to theirs. I ran away to sea after Dad died, and I got up and did my first ever arena concert after Mum went. I carried on living my life as they would have wanted me to and, as devastating as it was to say goodbye to both of them, at least I could do so without also grieving a future planned with them. I was an independent woman, making my own way in the world, but with Ed it was not like that at all. My life was intertwined with his and my future was *our* future, together.

I found myself reflecting a lot on Mum's passing after I lost Ed. She was incredibly stoical, and when she was in the hospice I never once heard her complain. On the contrary, she said many times, 'It's all going to be fine.' That was a comfort to us all. Mum was at peace at the end, and that helped everyone in the family to cope with saying goodbye. I thought Mum was leaving a few days before she passed, because she was so calm and still it was as if she was in a coma. 'Why isn't she going?' I wondered. I had a chair at the side of Mum's bed and I sat there day and night, stroking her hair and putting my hand on her head, to reassure her she wasn't alone. After four days of this, one of the nurses at the hospice asked me to step outside the room for a minute, and it was only then that Mum finally passed.

Oh my God, I had been keeping her.

My hand on her head was meant to reassure her, but I realised that in fact I was holding her back, sending the message: 'Don't you dare leave me.' I was devastated when I worked this out, but the nurses reassured me that I mustn't worry or feel any guilt about it. I had done what I felt was best, and when someone you love is dying you must follow your heart and do what feels right. The nurses and all the staff were so experienced and so kind, and at times like that you have to trust that they will be the hand that leads you.

* * *

The other day I sat at the piano, practising some of the numbers for my upcoming tour, *With All My Love*. For the first time ever, I'm going to be playing 'The Hand That Leads Me' on the piano, rather than just singing it, and I want to be able to play it effortlessly, because I know a lot of my energy will be going into holding it all together on stage. Sue was stood beside me, listening quietly, as I practised on my piano in the living room at home.

'Right, I think I'm getting there,' I said. 'What d'you think?'

When I turned to look at Sue she had tears streaming down her face, and that were it. I started crying too, and I couldn't stop. 'How the flipping heck am I going to play this on the tour?' I said, trying to laugh through my tears. I'm still wondering that. After taking the antidepressants for two years, I gradually weaned myself off them in the summer of 2023. Now I can feel all my emotions again, thank God, but I have so much crying to catch up on, I really do.

I've made a lot of progress in the last three years. Every night when I get into bed, and every morning when I wake up, the fact Ed is not there still hits me like a punch in the stomach. I'm ready for it now. Instead of focusing on my loss, I make myself think about how lucky I was to share the precious time I did with Ed. I remember happy times, like eating at our favourite Italian, or when he pushed me on a swing. I also remind myself that my life today, and my future, is all set up because of him and the foundations we laid together. I have a diary that I write in every day. It does me good to write about everything and then let it go. I'm old school and also keep my appointments in there, and in the morning I try to write down all the things I'm grateful for, which helps me start the day with a positive mindset.

Ed would have wanted me to live a life full of joy, and that is what I try to do, every day, even with the simplest things. When I sit down on my own to watch TV, I'm grateful to be in charge of the remote, and when I read a book in bed, I'm thankful I have the luxury of being able to keep the light on for as long as I want.

We're all blessed to have time on this earth and every day should be an adventure of some kind, whether that's losing yourself in a good book or doing something on a bigger scale. I remind myself all the time that happiness is in my hands and I can choose to be happy and to look for positives, even when bad things happen. I am also very aware that I am not the only person grieving, far from it, and I remind myself to look outwards and think of others.

As Benjamin Franklin said, nothing is certain except death and taxes. That's the reality of life, unfortunately. All of us are only on this earth for so long and we only have so many summers left, so we *have* to make the most of them. I used to tell Ed that I intend to knee-slide into death with a bottle of champagne in one hand, and that on my tombstone I want it written: 'She flew by the seat of her pants.' He laughed, and I know that he'd love the fact I still stand by both of those things today.

I still have bad days, of course I do, but I'm kind to myself when they happen, and I give myself some slack. 'We all have 'em,' I tell myself. 'Today is not a good day, but don't worry, tomorrow will be a better day.' I always let myself experience my grief when it hits me, because as I've said, we have to let it out. We are not meant to hold on to such strong and sad emotions; if you do I think it makes you ill. At funerals, people often hold it together until the music comes on at the end of the service. Then the tears start to flow, and that is the healthy release everybody needs.

When I'm on stage I'm not afraid to talk about losing Ed, or my mum, and when I do I always see people in the audience drying their eyes. That's a good thing. If my music gives other people an outlet for their own emotions, we're connecting with each other, and that's what it's all about. I'm so thankful to everyone who has ever sung along, waved a torch and just been there at my concerts, because that's what's got me through, it really has. Those people gave *me* permission to grieve, and it was a privilege to do the same for them, sending that big wheel out into the audience and watching it spin back to me.

There is no end. After you lose someone you don't move on, you move forward. My dad is still with me all these years on, and so is my mum. Instead of being sad, I think about all the gifts they gave me in my life, and how they helped me move forward, then and now. It's the same with Ed. Even if I meet someone else, he will be with me, always. Even when it's my turn to take it nice and slow – hopefully a very long time from now.

CHAPTER EIGHT

FINDING YOUR PEOPLE

'People come into our lives for a reason'

'I've never laughed as much,' I said to Sue. 'It's been fabulous, it really has.'

We'd rung in 2024 at a Scottish lodge with a group of girl pals, and it had been one of the best New Year's Eves I'd ever spent.

My relationship with my female friends has changed for the better since losing Ed, and I don't think that's unusual. When you have a partner and you work hard, you need to prioritise each other when you have time off. That's what I always did when Ed was alive, and though I didn't ever want to compromise my relationships with friends, my busy life meant I didn't spend as much time with them as I wished I could.

There's a certain amount of freedom that comes with being single, and I'm making the most of it. 'Shall we nip up to the Italian tonight?' one of the girls might say, and I love that I can just go out without consulting anybody else. I go out an awful lot more than I did before, and when I had the chance to spend New Year's Eve with my friends, I was delighted. Off we went to Scotland with a bottle of whisky, and we spent the evening having a few drams and playing the card game UNO! We all went into the street just before midnight and watched fireworks, which were magical, and a piper played as we counted down to the new year. After that it was back to the lodge to be welcomed by a roaring fire and a Rusty Nail cocktail we'd made for a treat, with Scotch whisky and Drambuie. Then we finished off the card game and turned in – how fabulous! That's my kind of night, and I enjoyed myself so much. I like to have a chat, and UNO! is one of those games you can keep playing while you talk. It's great to curl up and watch a boxset when you're on your own, but when you're with friends it's nice to switch off from screens, phones included, if you can. We had such a hoot that night, and now whenever we got out locally we often take a pack of cards along. Simple pleasures, that's what I like.

✳ ✳ ✳

My gran always said, 'you don't need a lot of stuff to enjoy yourself', and I learned how true that is from a very young age, on a holiday I've never forgotten. It was the year Dad was recovering from his accident down the mine and he wasn't able to drive us to the Yorkshire coast, where we usually went on holiday every year. Mum thought it would break

Dad's heart if we went to Bridlington without him, as he loved it there so much, and Janet had started working in Tesco and was quite happy to stay home with him. The upshot was that Mum and Gran decided to take Tony and me to Monifieth on the Scottish coast, where Gran grew up.

The happy memories I have of that holiday have stayed with me for life, and Tony and I still laugh our heads off when we reminisce about what happened before we even got to our caravan site. After taking a train to Dundee we caught a local bus along the coastal road, and a few minutes after the bus pulled away a car started flashing and beeping behind us. The bus driver obstinately ignored the car for mile after mile, even when the flashing and beeping became more and more urgent and the man at the wheel was waving frantically. When the bus driver finally relented and pulled over, the car screeched to a halt behind us and the motorist jumped out, holding something aloft triumphantly.

'Look!' Tony and I said, recognising the prize straight away. 'It's Gran's suitcase!'

For some reason Gran's case was round, like a giant hat box, and it must have rolled out of the luggage space under the stairs of the bus, where it had been placed on its side by the driver. Then it obviously kept on rolling, down the street. *I ask you!* Tony and me were in stitches, we really were.

When we got to Monifieth there was nothing there but sand dunes and fresh air, and it really was heavenly. Mum would walk to the bakery every morning and we'd wake up to the smell of bacon and egg rolls being cooked. Straight after breakfast me and Tony were off, spending the whole day running around the dunes, flying a kite and playing games on the sand. He's a lovely soul, is Tony. I was only seven and he was 12, but he didn't once let our age gap get in the way.

On an evening we went to the chip shop for fish suppers, black pudding and chips, and the local speciality of white pudding, made with sausage, oatmeal and suet. After that it was back to the caravan, where the gas lamps were lit and we played cards and chatted until we dropped. There were no phones and no TV – we didn't even have electricity – and what sheer joy that was.

* * *

An appreciation of the simple pleasures in life is just one of the many things Gran taught me. She'd had a tough start in life, had our Gran. Her mother was unmarried when she fell pregnant to a local boy in the early 1900s and, passing her child off as her little sister, she left Gran to be raised up by an older gentleman she knew well and trusted, who lived in a cottage overlooking the sea in Monifieth. We don't know much more about this man, except that Gran called him 'Grandpa', he looked after her well and she loved him dearly. Still, I don't think Gran ever forgave her mother for what she did. My great-grandmother then went to work as a nanny for a wealthy family, a job that took her all round the world and hardly ever back to Scotland, or to our grandmother.

Gran embodied determination and resilience, just like my dad. She went on to have four children but was widowed in 1950, at the age of 45. By all accounts Gran kept the family afloat by taking in extra washing. She also baked, something she was so good at that during the war the neighbours in her tenement building used to give her their rations, asking her to make cakes and scones and fresh bread for them. Gran certainly knew which side her bread was buttered, and when her three oldest children and their families – including Mum, Dad and baby Janet – told her they were relocating to Wakefield in the mid 1950s, my grandmother made a snap decision to go with them, bringing with her my Aunt Barbara, the youngest of the four siblings.

Everybody lived on the same street, packed into two tiny terraced houses in a very run down part of Wakefield, but they were together, and that's what mattered. If there was any silver lining to come from Gran's sad history, this was it.

She knew the value of family, and though it broke her heart to leave Scotland in her middle age, being with her loved ones was what counted. She was so proud of each and every one of us, and I'll never forget what she said after she came to see my first ever theatre performance, at the Opera House in Blackpool, in 1998. 'I just lived for this day,' she said as we sipped champagne in the dressing room after the sell-out show. 'All I wanted was to see you be a star.' Gran was well into her nineties then and, oh my goodness, if there was ever a moment when I knew the importance of close family bonds, that were it.

* * *

When I was travelling here, there and everywhere, making all of my cruising and holiday programmes, I always looked forward to coming back home to Wakefield. It didn't matter which wonders of the world I'd seen, or how many once-in-a-lifetime experiences I'd enjoyed, being away for long periods of time always reminded me how lucky I was to come from this fabulous Yorkshire city. That's never changed. I count my blessings every day that I still live in the same place I grew up, where I'm surrounded by family, friends and familiarity. Wakefield is where I belong, and coming home is like returning to my safe place, somewhere I can rest and recuperate and recharge, ready for the next adventure.

I've always appreciated the fact Wakefield is in the middle of the country and I can get anywhere in the UK within hours. It's surrounded by the beauty of the Yorkshire Dales – Denby Dale is stunning and just up the road – and yet Leeds is only 20 minutes away, for all the fabulous shopping and everything else a thriving city has to offer. I can visit *anywhere* in Yorkshire and still sleep in my own bed at night, surrounded by my home comforts. No packing. No passport control. No dodgy tummy. No jet lag. I know the name of my local butcher and there's an Asda just up the road from me. Priceless!

When I married Henrik, refusing to move to London was one of my better decisions, if not the best. It was instinctive, and I'm very glad I listened to my heart. After our marriage fell apart I wouldn't have lasted five minutes on my own down south, fancy house or not. I'd have been running back up the M1 to Silcoates Street like a rat up a drainpipe. I've always needed to be amongst my people, and life has shown me time and again how important friends and family are, especially when the going gets tough.

The friends I made at school were a great counter-weight to all the bullies I encountered, making my life not just bearable, but fun. I met Liz at St Michael's Middle School, and she was a brilliant friend, and someone I spent so much time with that Mum would say, 'When you've seen one, you've seen t'other!' We had another friend, Gail, and on the walk to school I'd call for Liz first and then Gail would join us halfway through the journey. Oh, the good old days when everyone walked to school! Liz was younger than me, so when I moved up to Thornes House Secondary School she didn't join me until a couple of years later. We remained friends, though, and after we left school we used to go jiving at the Mecca every Monday night, which I loved.

I met Jane and Mandy at Thornes House, and they were also great pals. They were both lovely girls, the kind I could talk to about anything, and who I felt safe to be myself with. That's the key, isn't it? We all need friends who love us for who we are, and who share in our successes, support our dreams and make us feel good about ourselves, come what may.

I have nothing but fond memories of Liz, Gail, Jane and Mandy, though we are no longer in touch. The fact we went our separate ways is no reflection on the friendships we shared. School friends grow up and drift apart, and that's a pattern that repeats throughout our lives. People come into our lives for a reason, and I believe very strongly that they leave when they're meant to. That's why I never worry when friendships end. Whether you're breezing though life or battling through storms, there will always be different passengers climbing on board your ship, just as there will always be others heading for the port, leaving you to sail off on new journeys without them.

Wendy was another friend I made when I moved up to Thornes House, along with Caroline, a lovely person and a life-long pal. I didn't see much of Wendy immediately after I left school because I was working all week in my office job and I was out most nights, whether I was dancing at the Mecca with Liz, ballroom dancing with my dad or going to the Balne Lane club with Mum and Dad on the weekend. However, as fate would have it one Thursday night Wendy turned up at Alverthorpe Club, on the outskirts of Wakefield, with some members of her family. I was there ballroom dancing with Dad, and after that night Wendy started to come to the club regularly, often taking it in turns to dance with my dad, as he was such a fabulous dancer.

A few months down the line, Wendy arrived to find me laughing at the bar with Tony, who she'd never met before.

He's always been a looker, has Tony, and Wendy made a jokey remark about how I always got the best-looking blokes. 'What?' I said, spitting out my Coke. 'You're welcome to him – he's my big brother!' Tony and Wendy have been married for more than 40 years and are as close as ever, and they are fantastic grandparents now too. Some things are written in the stars, and I'm so happy they found each other, not least because I couldn't have asked for a better sister-in-law.

Wendy and I are the very best of friends. If anything's going wrong, she's the one to turn to, because she's always willing to help and if she says she'll do something, it gets done. And as annoying as it is, while she's watching your back and looking after everybody else, she always looks glamorous, the house is immaculate and she'll magic a three-course dinner onto the table!

Tony and Wendy now live a stone's throw from my house, and Janet is five minutes away. I love that they are all nearby. As three siblings we each have a very different outlook on life, but we're closer than we've ever been. In some families, adversity creates rifts, but in ours the opposite has been true. I think everything we have been through over the years, especially losing Mum, has brought us closer together.

I feel very blessed. I know not everybody is lucky enough to have a good family around them, although as I learned at school, even when you think you are the odd one out, destined to be on your own, there are always kind people out there who can become your friends and allies. My advice is that if you don't have a good family, go out and find yourself a new one. I'm a great believer in that. There is no law to say you have to stick with family come what may. We've all heard the phrase 'blood is thicker than water', but if you are unable to have a happy, healthy relationship with your blood relatives, I think it's far better for everyone if you find yourself a new family of people, one that brings you joy.

If you're lucky, a new group finds you, and sometimes the right people come along at just the right time in your life. The Loose Women did just that for me, and what a fabulous gang it was to be in. The first time I went on the show I was blown away by how much love was in the room, and how supportive everybody was, not just of me as a nervous guest, baring my soul about the breakdown of my marriage, but of each other. I wasn't expecting that and it was such a pleasant surprise. When I returned as a regular panelist it was like going home, it really was. And what a pleasure it was to be in a position where people wanted to know what I thought, rather than telling me to keep my gob shut!

During my ten years on the show I would work with the most amazing women, and it was fabulous. It felt like the Loose Women became my bezzie mates overnight, and the same was true as different panelists joined in subsequent years. I can't remember a time when I wasn't at ease in their company, laughing my head off with them and trusting them with my secrets. I came in for a lot of stick on that show, mostly for still living with my mother in my forties, but I never minded. That was the beauty of the format. We were all at ease with one another and we got on so well we could say anything to each other, knowing that nobody would take offence, because no offence was ever meant. I think that's a sign of true friendship.

We socialised quite a lot outside of work, and I loved that. Honestly, forget the fact we'd just come out of the ITV studio on the South Bank, where *Loose Women* was filmed. When a group of us walked into a bar we might as well have stepped off the set of *Sex and the City*. 'Oh my God, it's the Loose Women!' people would say, heads turning and cameras flashing. We all thought it was hilarious that anyone looked twice at us, because the whole point was we could have been any other group of female friends, going out for a drink and a giggle together. That was the genius of the show, because the producers made it so we could capture that same vibe on screen.

Nights out with the Loose Women always reminded me of when I worked in Pussycat, and everyone from the centre bar would go out to a fancy club at Walton Hall. 'Oh God, they're here!' people said as we bowled up, always fizzing with energy. Without fail, every time we walked in I thought I was in a scene from *Dirty Dancing*. We were no Patrick Swayzes or Jennifer Greys, but we could all hold our own on the dance floor and we'd really go for it. I absolutely *loved* those nights. It wasn't about the attention; it was a fabulous feeling to be in a group of people I really bounced off, fitted in with and could be myself with.

I'd been working on *Loose Women* for four years when I met Ed again and, given that our reunion took place in the ITV studios, the girls on set knew all about it from day one. Though I knew in my heart that Ed was the right man for me, I didn't have a good track record when it came to relationships, and of course at that point Ed was still in The Searchers, touring all over the world. Lynda Bellingham joined *Loose Women* in 2007, and we had become good pals. One day, very early on in my relationship with Ed, I confided to Lynda that however much I wanted it to work with Ed, and however good we were together, I was afraid of history repeating itself.

'What do you think?' I asked. 'Should I be doing this? I'm not sure it's the right thing.'

Lynda told me she'd have to meet him before she gave me an answer. I really valued her opinion, and so I arranged for the three of us to have dinner together one night when Ed was on a day off and could meet us in London. To my surprise, we'd barely sat down when Lynda went straight for the jugular.

'So, what are your intentions towards my friend?' she asked.

I'll never forget her asking Ed that. It took my breath away, it really did. It was as if she was interviewing him for a blinking job!

Ed passed with flying colours, of course. Lynda thought he was lovely, and the next day she told me not to let this one go – he was a keeper. When the other Loose Women met Ed they all loved him too, which was very important to me, as they were my best mates at the time, they had centuries of experience between them (sorry, ladies!) and their opinions mattered. Ed was well aware he was under the microscope and he thought it was all very funny. 'Blimey,' he said, 'I *have* passed a test if I've got past the Loose Women. First Lynda, then a panel interview! Do you want references?'

Unfortunately, despite all the vetting and caution on my part, I did have a wobble, a bit later on in our relationship. It happened after Ed and I tried and failed, three times, to go on holiday. We'd been together for well over a year and were engaged, but I started to fear the worst: history *was* repeating itself. Ed had done 250 gigs in our first 12 months together, and that was the norm. Did I want to spend my life living apart from my fiancé? I loved Ed dearly, but if he was never there, was there any point in carrying on? One day, in February 2010, I woke up on my own – again – and decided the answer was no.

Ed had been away for weeks on end, touring in Australia. I took the bull by the horns and phoned him up, telling him this wasn't working for me. Ed was very taken aback, and immediately started to talk about what we could do to make things work. I realised this was what I wanted to hear. I didn't want to end things with Ed, I just wanted to stop being apart from him. Unfortunately, in the middle of our conversation I heard another phone ringing in the background. Given that it was very late at night in Australia and my emotions were already running high, that tipped me over the edge. Who the hell was calling him at this time? I told Ed I was sorry, this wasn't working. And then I put the phone down and felt my heart break.

When I went into the *Loose Women* studios the next day I wasn't in a good place at all. A producer said, 'Happy Valentine's Day!' and I couldn't respond. I hadn't realised it was 14 February, and that was the last thing I wanted to hear. I desperately didn't want to lose Ed, but there was no choice: I'd come to the conclusion The Searchers' jam-packed diary had made the decision for us. I was in agony. The other Loose Women had been so supportive of our relationship, and this would come as such a shock. I couldn't face telling anyone what had happened, and so I kept everything bottled up.

As it turned out, it's just as well I kept my mouth shut for once. *Loose Women* had got Ed to film a special Valentine's message for me, on Sydney Bridge, telling me he loved me and would be home soon. I was mortified when I discovered the ringing phone had been a member of our team, checking with Ed that everything had gone to plan. When they screened Ed's message all I could say was 'Oh God', and start to cry. It was very obvious to my friends that something had gone badly wrong. Carol McGiffin asked me what the matter was, while Sherrie Hewson's jaw dropped as she said 'Oh, dear.'

All's well that ends well. It was thanks to that peculiar chain of events that I sat down with Ed and thrashed out what we needed to do to stay together, because despite what I'd said in that phone call, that's what both of us wanted. It was very obvious by now that for our relationship to survive we had to learn our lesson from 30 years earlier, and one of us needed to stop work. I loved Ed so much I was prepared for that to be me, but Ed had made up his mind. He was ready for retirement, and though he would miss being in The Searchers, it was time to put our relationship first. It would be a big change, but as I always say, you have to embrace change; that's how you grow.

Ed made new friends, of course. He got to know everyone in my band and sometimes he joined me when I did TV and other work, which was great. One of the best times was when I was appearing in *Cats*, a role I have to thank Lynda for, albeit in a roundabout way. Lynda was a seasoned panto performer, and she often said I should give it a go. 'No, it's not for me,' I always said. It looked like a lot of hard work to me, and all around Christmas – and I absolutely *love* Christmas.

I changed my mind after Lynda was diagnosed with bowel cancer in 2013, and then her prognosis became unexpectedly terminal the following year. It was utterly devastating news. From the start I had told her to just say the word if I could do anything at all to help, and in September 2014 she had a favour to ask: would I consider taking over her role as the good fairy in *Jack & The Beanstalk*, at the Birmingham Hippodrome?

From that moment on, everything happened so quickly. It was a great honour to step into Lynda's shoes but, unbelievably, by the time I started the run, my dear friend had passed away. She was only 66; it was so hard to take in. Throughout the run we had Lynda's picture on the wall backstage at the theatre, and it really did feel like she was watching over us the whole time. It was so tough carrying on with the show every day, but we all knew that Lynda would have wanted us to have a ball, and we did – thankfully you can't not have fun doing panto. We put our hearts and souls into putting on between ten and 12 shows a week for six weeks, though it really took its toll on me. I was completely exhausted after the final performance, both physically and emotionally, and I vowed never to do panto again.

Lynda had been an incredibly hard worker all through her life and had an amazing career, but she also knew the importance of family, and of nourishing her relationships with the people who matter. At her funeral, in November 2014, the packed pews and the palpable love in the church were testament to how deeply Lynda cherished her loved ones, and how special she was to so many people. That day I thought back to how Lynda would often remind me that Ed was a good man, and that I needed to look after what we had together. I listened to her words; she was a very wise woman.

Towards the end of the panto run my agent, Craig Latto, came to see the show and I told him I was going to take time off. 'When in doubt, do nowt' is a phrase I grew up hearing, and this was one of those times when I knew I should stop and take a breath before deciding what to do next. I was always going to go on tour again, but what else did I want to do? *Loose Women* had undergone a revamp recently and had a newsier slant, and I had decided to step back. I'd had ten brilliant years on the show and the door was open if I wanted to pop in and out, but my days of being a regular panelist were over. It was an easy decision – I'm not a journalist and wouldn't have been comfortable giving my two penneth on current affairs – and it meant I'd have more time for whatever came along next.

As soon as the panto ended, my immediate priority was to spend some quality time at home with Ed, and to see more of my mum and the rest of my family. When Craig asked me how much time I was taking off, I told him a year. That made his eye bulge for a second, but Craig would never stand in my way of anything, and he always backs me when I listen to what my body is telling me.

I can't tell you how good it felt to head back to Wakefield. It felt like weights were lifting off me with every mile I drove up the M1, and when I walked in my front door relief and gratitude flooded over me. 'I'm home!' I said, and I loved hearing those words bounce off the walls. Having time off, on home soil, was going to be just the tonic I needed.

I had six relaxing weeks before Craig called me with the very exciting news that I'd been asked to audition for *Cats*. 'Oh God!' I thought, my heart leaping. 'I can't turn that down, can I?' Craig explained that I would need to audition in front of Sir Andrew Lloyd Webber himself, as well as other leading lights of musical theatre, including the director Sir Trevor Nunn, who wrote the lyrics. 'Oh God!' I thought again. It was a terrifying prospect, but this was the opportunity of a lifetime.

When I was told I'd won the role I was ecstatic. This was a huge vote of confidence from the upper echelons of the industry, and I knew that if I pulled it off, it would finally put paid to all the critics who still saw me as 'just' a cruise ship singer who got lucky. One of the lovely things about getting *Cats* was that the producer, David Ian, had seen me in *Jack & The Beanstalk*, and he spotted that I had the stamina to perform up to 12 shows a week. *Cats* was eight shows a week, and it was full-on as I also had to dance, but I'd proven I could stay the course for the duration of a run. It all felt meant. None of this would have happened without Lynda, the original good fairy, and I was so grateful to her for opening the first door for me.

I had Lynda to thank for a lot more besides. Even though I suddenly wasn't having as much time off I planned, I had loved my six weeks at home and was already feeling recharged. That said, I had watched and learned so much from Lynda, and I was determined not to undo the good work. Spending time with Ed was *so* important, and instead of going to Blackpool on my own and staying in a hotel when I did *Cats*, I talked Ed into coming with me and renting a house. 'The shed will still be there when you get back, love,' I told him. 'Go on, then,' he said, rolling his eyes.

We found a fabulous Airbnb that we used as our base throughout the season and we had the best time, we really did. It was summertime, there was a jacuzzi and a steam room and the house had loads of spare bedrooms. On Friday nights other members of the cast would come over for a glass of wine and a chill out in the hot tub, and we'd all be raring to go again for the Saturday matinée. I have nothing but happy memories of that summer, on stage and off. Ed and I had learned another valuable lesson. It's very important to set out your stall in a relationship, but you also need to know when to move the boundaries. Just talk it through, and you might find that mixing things up a bit makes both of you happier. Having Ed with me on that job was absolutely one of those times. We both loved it, although I reckon Ed must have missed his shed more than I bargained for, because we ended up with three sheds in the garden after that!

One of the many things I loved about *Loose Women* was that I never felt I had to compete for my place at the table. The opposite was true. Despite all the ribbing that went on, nobody was trying to outdo or belittle anybody else. We were all in it together, supporting and championing each other. That's a gift we gave each other, and it's one I took with me into my music, when Martin and I were beefing up the shows and tours. As well as hiring the very best people we could afford, we took on band members who had the same outlook as us, wanted to be part of our family and who connected well with each other. And that's when it all started to come together.

I feel so blessed to have my band around me. When Martin first suggested he took over as tour manager, Ed immediately told me to go for it. 'I trust him, let him fly,' he said. Martin has vision and ambition and he has grown in an amazing way; I absolutely would not be doing my next tour with Live Nation if it weren't for him. To watch someone flourish is so lovely, and Martin's success has rubbed off on the whole lot of us. That's what happens when you work with the best people – you all get better, together.

I feel lifted up by every member of the band. They all make me feel safe on stage, we have a great laugh and we all work our socks off to put on the best show. Our guitarist, Steve, is not only a very talented guy but is also a lovely person, great company and as solid as a rock. He's also a big family man, which I love. We've been working with each other since 2008, and I know I can always depend on him. Funnily enough, a long time ago I had a dream in which Steve walked over and kissed the top of my head, telling me he would always have my back. I've never forgotten it, and it confirmed everything I felt about him.

As I've mentioned, it was Steve who recommended Seán Barry as our fabulous MD. Seán also plays keyboards, and is another indispensable member of our family, one who feels like he's always been there even though he was the last one to join the party. Then there's Jim Pitchforth, on percussion and vocals. What can I say? Jim lives around the corner from me, he's another big family man and I've also known him for years. You know Jim can do the job brilliantly, and he always has good energy around him, and the same is true of Jamie Little, our fantastic drummer. It's thanks to Ed that we have Jamie on board. Ed saw him performing in Blackpool years ago and told me straight away: 'You need him.' I listened – Ed had not only drummed for Liquid Gold and The Searchers, but for a decade in between he was the drummer in Mud. I couldn't have asked for a better talent scout, could I? And Ed was spot on about Jamie – he's fabulous at what he does, and he fits right in. When the band is together we bring out the very best in each other and have a great time. That's where the magic lies, because without joy and camaraderie on stage you can't spin that wheel and send the love and energy out to the audience.

*   *   *

Just as there are some friends you drift apart from, there are others you don't see for a while and then 'poof' they're back, a bit like a fairy godmother. Janice is one of those. She saw potential in me when I was a teenager working at Casanova's, and though I didn't see it then as clearly as I do now, she was a very influential person in my life. 'Jane, can you just get up and sing?' she used to say when I was running the VIP bar, because she knew I had it in me, and she wanted to bring me on. Then before I knew it she was asking me to help with PR and putting together the dance troupe, neither of which I'd have done without her encouragement. Janice is a very intuitive person, interested in the spiritual world, and when I look back, it's as if she's been another hand that leads me, coming into my life and giving me the push in the right direction just when I needed it. She was there when things were going wrong with Henrik, for instance, when she tactfully told me that I should be earning the type of money that could buy a posh house in London. That had been enough to make my ears prick up and have me hot-footing it back to Wakefield to look at my accounts, but before I left Janice told me something else too. 'You'll think I'm so weird,' she said, 'but I had your gran visit in the night, and she said "go and look at the books".' *Blimey.*

I've lost touch with more friends than I've kept, but Janice has always been there, one way or another, even if some years we only manage a Christmas card. Years ago she invited me to her husband's 50th birthday party in Marbella, and I took my sister Janet with me. Back in the day, Janice and Mike had turned Casanova's into one of the most successful clubs in Europe (famous for a while for having telephones on the tables, so you could call another table if you fancied someone!) and they've never stopped being successful in all their subsequent ventures. Cilla was at Mike's party in Marbella – they knew her because they were neighbours with Cliff Richard – and I found myself sitting next to her. *It's Cilla!* I couldn't believe it, and I was so starstruck I could barely speak. We only exchanged a few pleasantries, but it was such an honour to meet her. Janice knew how I felt about Cilla, and this was another moment that propelled me forward. She was one of my childhood idols, and the more I learned about the industry, the more respect and admiration I had for Cilla. When she started out it was a man's world, but she didn't take any prisoners and she knew her worth. Cilla was a pioneer for women in television and I will always be thankful to her for paving the way for the rest of us even though, let's be honest, there are still not enough women fronting primetime shows. Cilla also achieved something not many people pulled off, myself included, and that was having her husband, Bobby, as her manager. What a role model she was. I looked at Janice that night with a heart full of gratitude. She hadn't had to do any of the things she had done for me over the years, but she'd given me so many opportunities, and she had been instrumental in keeping my dreams alive, and helping them come true.

✳ ✳ ✳

It's no accident that I started this chapter by writing about Sue, and I'm ending it by writing about her too because, like Wendy, Sue's been there for me through everything, and she's still very much here, and isn't going anywhere! Sue moved in with me in 2022, after she split up from her fiancé. It made sense. Having completed the building work, the house was plenty big enough for Sue to have her side and me to have mine, and we could be company for each other. Mind you, she's hardly ever in. She's like a whirling Dervish, is Sue – I don't know where she gets her energy from.

'Who'd have thought we'd be here, like this, like two bookends,' Sue laughed the other day. She's made some fantastic chicken noodle soup and we were sitting at the breakfast bar, enjoying a big bowlful each. 'By God this is good,' I said. 'You do know the only reason I asked you to move in is because I can't cook?'

'Give over,' she said. 'Your cheese on toast is, well, edible . . . !'

It's dead easy to be with Sue, and it should be, given the length of time we've known each other.

Asking her to join me when it all went bonkers after *The Cruise* is another one of my best decisions. Very sadly, Sue's sister June had recently passed away, aged just 52, from bone cancer. Sue and I had talked about forming a duo, but when I suddenly hit the big time she was very happy to be the backing vocalist. There is no ego with Sue. She'd do a huge show with me and my band one night and then a gig on her own in a working men's club the next. 'Live from the London Palladium!' it said on the chalkboard outside a pub in Grimsby one time. I don't think people believed it, but it was true.

Sue was the only person who stood up and said 'who are these people?' and 'what are they doing to you?' when the London lot tried to turn me into somebody I wasn't. It was exactly what I was thinking, and I'd have felt even more isolated I didn't have Sue there, validating my reaction. She was also a great person to have around when I was having trouble with Henrik. One night, Sue and I went to watch the filming of *An Audience With . . .* Henrik was always very professional, and late nights and alcohol were frowned upon when I had work the next day, which was basically all the time. On this particular night, I just thought 'sod it, I'm letting my hair down for once'. Sue and I were having such a great time, chatting to Paul O'Grady and meeting Graham Norton and some of the people he worked with. Everything was making me laugh, up until the moment Sue looked at her phone and told me Henrik was waiting outside. Sue understood my frustrations with

Henrik's management style, but even so she tried her best to keep things running smoothly between us. On that occasion she did it by kicking me in the ankle and telling me to shut up when she finally got me in the back of car! Another time, I'd had a falling-out with Henrik before a gig in Nottingham.

'What am I going to do,' I wailed to Sue. 'Henrik and me aren't even talking. How am I going to do this gig?'

Sue looked me straight in the eye. 'Jane, you've been a singer all your life. You've gone to gigs on your own. You've put your own gear up. What are you so afraid of? Let's just go and do it. What do you need him there for?'

'He's my manager, he's my husband,' I said. 'He has to be there. What am I going to do?'

Despite having very different characters, Sue and Henrik got on okay. She could see he was only trying his best and she never interfered or criticised him. However, seeing me quivering and fretting like this really got her back up. When we worked in the clubs, Sue always said I was the fearless one, the trailblazer. I'd get new lighting and everyone else would have to up their game, or I'd be the first to call out the pub owner who didn't pay properly, or failed to deal with drunks. Now I was a pathetic mess, and Sue saw red. And when Sue sees red, she can have quite a potty mouth, let me tell you.

'What are you going to do?' she repeated back to me. 'Here's what you are going to do, Jane. Tell him to fuck off! Now come on, let's get to that gig!'

With that the pair of us set off like Thelma and Louise, cackling as we went. Sue was right, and she taught me something very useful that day. Isn't it funny how people make you think you need them, and actually you don't? Looking back, I spent far too many years thinking that I needed a man there to help me, whether it was my dad as my roadie, or when I needed a manager. But guess what, I *could* do it without a man, and that night in Nottingham turned out to be one of the best gigs in my entire life.

'That were just fabulous!' I said to Sue afterwards. 'I had the most amazing time!'

I'm not surprised I am still saying the same things to Sue all these years later. 'Isn't this fabulous?' I kept saying on New Year's Eve, during our lovely stay in the Scottish lodge. 'I'm having the best time ever.' I laughed so much that night that my stomach ached. Looking around at the other girl pals gathered around the UNO! board, a tot of whisky in hand and smiles on their faces, I counted my blessings. They were friends old and new, and right there and then, I was so lucky to have them all.

CHAPTER NINE

LEARNING TO LOVE YOURSELF

'What can I do for me today?'

'If you can't love yourself, how in the hell you gonna love somebody else?'

As a huge fan of *RuPaul's Drag Race*, I've heard this phrase hundreds of times over the years, though until recently I only really thought about it in terms of the drag queens on the show. That changed when I was invited to make a guest appearance on *RuPaul's Drag Race UK vs the World* at the start of 2024, and I heard Ru's signature rallying cry first-hand. 'That's such good advice for *everyone*,' I thought. 'How in the hell didn't I see it that way before?!'

We all need to learn to love ourselves, and we also need to keep on loving ourselves, and do a lot more of it. Not just so we can have happy relationships with other people, but so we can make the most of *everything* in life. It's no coincidence I finally tuned into RuPaul's message when I did – I had been lost in the wilderness for a long time since losing Ed, but I had finally climbed my way out of it.

It wasn't until the winter of 2023 that I recognised myself again when I looked in the mirror. 'Oh, you're back,' I thought one morning, my eyes lighting up as I looked at my reflection. Who knows why it happened on that particular day, but there I was, my old self, looking just like I used to, before the grief took over and everything went grey and fuzzy. I'd been shattered by Ed's death, but here I was, all stuck back together, at last. I felt elated, I really did.

We all have the capacity to love other people, and we usually do such a good job of looking after everybody else, don't we? My love for Ed, and for my mother, knew no bounds, and the same was true of how they loved me. My mother in particular was one of those people who was very good at loving everybody else, and after spending her whole life being the one who cared for others, she found it very hard to accept help from anyone, even when she was old and frail and really needed tending to. If I'd have told my mother she should learn to love herself more, she'd have chuckled and said she was doing just fine as she was, thank you. But I think if we're honest, we all need to take better care of ourselves, and the question 'what can I do for me today?' is one we should be asking every morning when we look in the mirror.

* * *

As soon as *The Cruise* put me on the map, I started travelling all over the country, doing my first tour and promoting my first album. I went on every chat show and visited every radio station that would have me, and between those interviews I was talking to journalists, stylists, record promoters and goodness knows who else from the back of the car, at airports and while I was waiting at railway stations. I was tired out but I kept going, even when my body was screaming at me to have a day off, look after myself better and get more sleep. It's what a lot of people do at the start of their career, and it wasn't going to go on for ever, I reasoned. I was making hay while the sun shone, and that seemed like the smart thing to do; the *only* thing to do.

The trouble was, it wasn't long before I started getting very irritable and upset. Henrik and I were having arguments for the first time in our relationship and – hands up – I was throwing strops and complaining when things weren't perfect. Yes, I did have my 'diva moments', and I don't mind admitting it. It wasn't that I saw myself as an actual diva, or someone who needed special treatment. Far from it – I was desperately trying to cling on to being the ordinary Yorkshire lass I was – though in those days, I was so focused on making a success of my career, there was no time for reflection or self-analysis. It was go, go, go, every day, and if I stopped, it would all come crashing down around me. At least, that's how it felt. I have a very different take on my behaviour now, and I can see that my anger and irritation were a response to sensory overload, stress and exhaustion – in other words, my 'diva moments' were the beginning of burnout.

When I look back through more experienced eyes, I can see that all my irritation and arguments should have been the red flags I needed to make me go 'hang on a minute, I'm going to go bang if this carries on'. As it was, it took me years and years to not just tune in, but to properly listen to what was happening to me, both physically and emotionally. Calling time on *Jane & Friends* in 2019 was huge progress for me. I'd got so wound up about the fact I always felt rushed, both because of my own manic schedule and the changing transmission dates, but thankfully, this time I listened to my body. I realised that things weren't right and something had to give, and once I took stock and realised how thinly I was spreading myself, and how busy and stressed I was in every area of my life, the decision to end the show came easily.

* * *

Though I didn't know it, I've been learning lessons about what I need to do for myself, and how to take care of *me*, my whole life long. As a child I used to find it really difficult to do my homework in the house, because the telly would be on in the living room and that was the only place where I could work, given that I shared a bedroom with my sister. I was very young when I started taking myself to the library across the road. Not being an academic child, I wasn't doing this for the love of studying. I enjoyed the solitude in the library, and that was the only place I could get it.

Quiet time to myself is something I've needed all through my life. When you choose to work on a cruise ship, and to entertain people for a living, there's often an assumption you're an extravert character with a limitless social battery. That's not necessarily the case. I need my 'me time', and I make no apology for that. If you want to have a chat, never sit next to me on a plane, because I'm no company at all. In go the earphones and out comes a good book. When I was a child, both Gran and Mum instilled in me that there's nothing better than having a good book to escape into, and I've been an avid reader throughout my life. When I'm reading a book on a plane, well, that's the ultimate dream, let me tell you! Nobody can phone me and I can't go anywhere until we touch down. I'm in another world entirely, and it's fabulous.

The Christmas after I lost Ed I got Covid, which was nowhere near as awful as it might sound. I adore *everything* about Christmas; it's my favourite time of the year. Me and Dad were the ones who always 'trimmed up', putting up the tree and decorating the house. There'd be so much tinsel and so many strings of lights that Silcoates Street would look like an explosion in Santa's grotto. I *loved* it. Mum was the cook and the dinner would be absolutely delicious. How she cooked a huge turkey and all the trimmings in our tiny kitchen, with no mod cons, I'll never know. And she always bought all the special things that still remind me of childhood Christmases: a metal tin of Quality Street, nuts you had to crack with nutcrackers, boxes of dried figs and Christmas crackers with terrible jokes. I'd get a small stocking from Father Christmas with a few things in, and there would be one main present from Mum and Dad. 'Here's the catalogue,' Mum would say. 'You can pick one toy you like and I'll get it for you.'

After Dad passed I kept up the tradition of doing all the trimming up at home, and I've carried it on, wherever I've been. I'm like Mrs Christmas now, and why not? It's Christmas, for goodness' sake, so you've got to spread some festive cheer. I spend days putting up massive trees in the kitchen and lounge, and hanging lights absolutely everywhere. When Ed was here, his brother would come up from Buckingham to stay for Christmas, and of course my family would be around. I looked forward to it so much, and we always had the best time, eating too much, having lovely winter walks and just chilling out.

'Have us round,' Mum used to say, 'and let us go!' That was her rule. 'You need your time to put your feet up and have a Baileys,' she'd tell me. 'I'll get home and get settled.' Mum always insisted on this, bless her, and I understood it was as much about her as it was about us, because she wanted to get back to watch all her soaps. I love that about getting older – people become much more comfortable about leaving the party early, and often it's the best thing for everybody.

I wasn't worried about my first Christmas without Ed. I was so tired out after doing the 2021 tour, I badly needed a rest and all I wanted was to stay in my own home and not do very much. I was very fortunate really, because when I realised I had Covid it was no hardship to me whatsoever. I didn't feel ill, and it meant I could be on my own without anybody feeling guilty, and without offending anyone. Wendy dropped me a dinner at the door and I popped it in the microwave, and I sat and watched Christmas films all day. Every year I watch *It's a Wonderful Life* and *White Christmas* and have a cry, though when I think about it, I didn't shed a tear this time, because of the antidepressants. Still, I enjoyed watching the old classics all the same; it's all about tradition for me, and I was perfectly content, on the sofa, in charge of the remote. It obviously wasn't the best Christmas on record, but I did appreciate having that time alone, and I counted my blessings that I was still here, in my lovely house, despite all I'd lost. I was unapologetically cut off from the world, and it was just what I needed. Mum had it right – we all need time to put our feet up and put our own needs first, and we should do more of it, without waiting for an excuse, or needing one.

* * *

In 2015, not long after I did *Cats*, I was asked if I wanted to take part in a reality show for ITV called *Sugar Free Farm*. My first reaction was 'thanks, but no, it's not for me'. The show involved living on a farm in Hampshire for three weeks, where my taste buds would be re-educated so I no longer wanted to eat sugar-laden foods. 'God forbid!' I thought. 'Life's to short not to have a scone.' I was a healthy size 14 and ate well enough, and after my experience in the dance troupe in Italy as a teenager, I'd vowed that nobody was ever putting me on a diet again. Over the years I'd taken great exception to people in the industry – and believe me, there have been *plenty* of them – who told me I'd look better if I lost some weight. Happily, when I learned the show was more about eating clean than losing weight, I thought again. I wanted as many healthy years in front of me as possible, and what was not to like about giving my body a detox, out in the English countryside? I signed up for the show.

The year before, when I was doing *Jack & The Beanstalk*, I lived on a lot of junk food, grabbing anything that was quick and easy, like pizzas, shop-bought sandwiches and chocolate bars. I needed instant fuel, but at the end of the day I was left feeling heavy and drained of energy. I actually ended up in bed for three days solid after the run finished, and there's no doubt my poor diet contributed to the depleted state I was in. At least I learned from that mistake when I did *Cats*, because I took a microwave to the theatre, and I bought healthy food from M&S that I could heat up. I was the oldest cast member there and I became quite the mother hen, making sure everyone ate properly before the show. 'It's so important,' I said. 'You need proper food or you'll start to flag!' I was like a broken record, though admittedly there was still room for improvement in my own diet, just like with most people, not least because we always had pizzas or takeaways and wine on our Friday hot tub nights.

It took two weeks on the farm for me to stop craving sugar, and I'm so glad I stuck with it. During that time we were up at sunrise every day, milking the cows and buffalo, we picked organic vegetables and we were taught how to make some fantastic sugar-free recipes. It was all so pleasant and wholesome, and I slept like a log every night. I lost about nine pounds in that first fortnight but, most importantly, I had more energy and felt so much better in myself. Thanks to the show's resident nutritionist, Angelique Panagos, I learned so many valuable lessons that have helped me have a better diet ever since. When I was hungry in the past, my default was always something carbohydrate-heavy, and I do love a pie. But I learned that when you eat a lot of carbs and processed foods, you're not nourishing your body properly, and so you still feel hungry. That's when you fill up on even more junk and end up feeling rubbish.

I was a model student when I left the farm, giving up white carbs completely and even making my own bread with wholemeal flour, seeds, oats and yoghurt. Cakes, crisps and biscuits all went too, and I discovered that once you give up sugar, your body goes off wine, because it's absolutely full of sugar and you're just not craving it anymore. I started having green smoothies for breakfast, packed with raw greens, seeds and banana, and probably the best tip I took from the farm was to always have a bowlful of chopped salad in the fridge, because if it's there, ready to eat, you're far more likely to have it over something else. As simple as it sounds, if you don't have unhealthy snacks in the house, you can't eat them, so I just stopped buying cakes and biscuits. I felt great and was proud of myself, but did I stick to it all long-term? Well, anyone who's seen me on *Gogglebox* already knows the answer is 'not entirely'! I love a glass of wine and a big bowl of crisps, and I make no apology for that. To my mind it's all about moderation, and my advice is to listen to the experts and make some positive changes, but don't feel you have to do it all. Doing the best you can is good enough, and if that means you cut out half the rubbish you had before, you're doing well. Life really is too short not to have a scone if you fancy one – just don't eat them every day. When it comes to alcohol, I'd much rather have one glass of really good wine than a whole bottle of something cheap. I love a glass of champagne at a wedding or a few drinks with the girls too, and there's nothing wrong with that.

My habits have changed in other ways over the years, and nowadays I only eat when I'm hungry. Like a lot of people my age, I was brainwashed into thinking we have to have three meals a day, but I've stopped all that. I don't have strict rules about fasting for a certain length of time, but what works for me is to skip breakfast and have one hot meal a day, usually made by Sue, who's a fabulous cook. Over the years I've taught myself how to cook all the foods my mother used to make, like beef stew, Yorkshire puddings and lamb chops with homemade gravy. As Mum used to say, if you can read, you can cook, and I'm not half bad. I just don't like cooking very much, and Sue is better at it, so she's the one with the pinny on most nights. Luckily we have very similar tastes and we're both plain eaters. We are meat, two veg and gravy girls, and it's always fresh meat from the local farm shop, where the butcher can tell us exactly where it came from. That's important to me. When I start eating, I eat like I've never eaten before, but when you're eating good, honest food, you can do that, guilt-free.

People are often surprised when I say I don't do any exercise, but it's true, at least not in terms of going to classes or playing sport. Active living is my thing – I love a walk and I use a lot of energy when I'm on tour, and that seems to be enough for me. I'm flattered when people assume I must go to the gym – I guess that shows I'm in decent shape, doesn't it? I've always been happy with my size and weight, and that's the most important thing of all. I feel full of energy now too, and best of all I never feel like I'm following any kind of regime, either with food or exercise. I strongly believe that's the key when it coms to eating well and staying fit and healthy. It all has to be sustainable and slot easily into your lifestyle, or you'll be miserable all the time and you'll give up.

On this year's tour I've decided to wear shorts. You heard me – shorts! Fancy that, a woman of my age! You know what, people can say what they like – if Kylie can do it, so can I. My legs have always been my best feature – and we all do have a best feature – and so I'm going to get them out. We should all show off our best bits with pride, no matter our age, and definitely without worrying what other people might think.

I have a rule when it comes to clothes: if I don't love it, and I don't feel good in it, I'm not wearing it. I think we all need to wear what we feel good in. Nothing else matters, and don't let anyone tell you that you can't wear something – age is only a number, and if it works for you, it works. The same is true of hair and make-up. I know what I like and I'm sticking with it. If anyone ever told me again to lose my big hair and start wearing 'more sophisticated' make-up, as they did in the noughties, I think I'd wallop them!

In the years when I was making all the travel shows, it was quite a mission getting my wardrobe sorted. I got a clothes budget, which was a fabulous perk, but it was over to me to choose all my outfits for every episode. Some days I'd be in three or four completely different situations, and I always wanted to look the part. 'You look great, Jane, and you can stay in what you've got on for the next thing,' I was told sometimes when we were filming. 'No!' I'd say. 'If I was on holiday, I wouldn't go out for dinner in this! I'm getting changed.' I like to look glam, and my clothes started to get a lot of attention from viewers, with people going on social media and talking about what I had on, and where my white jeans or colourful top came from. That was lovely, though it increased the pressure I put on myself to make sure every look was just right. Sue and I would spend two days solid preparing my clothes for every trip – it was a *huge* job – and we became quite the professionals when it came to holiday packing. If I had to pick three top tips, it's these: invest in packing cubes. They are indispensable – you don't even have to unpack. Never forget a laundry bag. And when it comes to cruising, elasticated slacks are your friend, especially for the second half of the trip!

I can't tell you how thankful and relieved I felt when a fabulous woman called Carol Capener got in touch with me a few years ago, explaining that she runs Carol C Collections, based in Leeds. 'Would you like me to supply clothes for you?' she asked. *Would I?* Oh my goodness, this was heaven sent! Sue and I went to Carol C's distribution warehouse and had a lovely two days selecting all of my clothes. The fact I was a size 12 sample size meant I could have my pick of absolutely everything, and I really can shop! It was absolutely brilliant, and it took so much pressure off me and Sue, as my whole wardrobe was done in one fell swoop. Mind you, I spent about four times my clothing allowance, but it was worth it. I was very happy, and it felt like a weight had been lifted, it really did. Clothes really should bring us joy, not stress, and Carol did me a huge favour.

Now the biggest problem I have when it comes to clothes is what to do with them all. I've got wardrobes galore in my house. I try to give stuff away to friends and family, if they fancy anything, and if something only gets worn once more and passed on again, or given to the charity shop, I'm delighted. My show outfits cost such a lot of money and so I make sure they get sold off for charity, which is another win-win. But I'm not trying to claim I'm a saint, because I'm not. My vice is online shopping – I'm a terror with it. It's so easy to get carried away, isn't it? And if I find something I love, I want to buy it in every colour. I've had to bring in a rule, and that is that if I buy something new, something's going out. Sue makes sure I stick to it, thank God. She's ruthlessly efficient with returns too, which is just as well, because I'm terrible at that part too. 'We're not keeping these!' Sue says. 'They're going back!' And off she goes to the post office, before they get lost in the back of a cupboard.

I've gone through different decades in terms of my style, and I think that's a natural thing to do. Along with the legs, my shoulders are the only other part of my body I class as 'best bits' these days. The rest – forget it, they can get covered up! I do like a jacket with good shoulder pads. It might sound very eighties, but for the more mature woman, a shoulder pad improves your posture, and when you stand tall it makes everything look better. For me a good blazer is a wardrobe essential – you can go to work in it or go out in it, and it looks great with a good pair of jeans. And by good jeans I mean ones with a bit of stretch in them, so you can move without cutting yourself in half.

I've been enjoying chunky jumpers lately and, of all the clothes, they really are a 'mood', wrapping you with warmth and comfort and making you feel safe and cosy. I love that, and I think that when you start to appreciate the impact clothes have on how you feel, you make better choices. Tuning in to your reaction to clothes also helps you develop your own look, and to discover what is 'you'. I'd love to design my own clothes, with the feel-good factor at the heart of them, because that is so important to me.

My mother was a woman who knew how to dress, and when I was 40, she told me it was time I started wearing 'foundation garments'. I was a bit affronted, if I'm honest.

Foundation garments? Me? I couldn't give a monkey's if I have a few lumps and bumps on display – we've all got 'em – but I have to say, Mum was right to give me a nudge. I discovered that shapewear can make a huge difference, especially under a long dress and the sort of gowns I wear on stage. And when you look fabulous, you feel fabulous, which is what it's all about.

* * *

When I travelled across Japan in 2023, making *Jane McDonald: Lost in Japan,* I witnessed a whole new way of living, which made me think.

'Let me do it!' Sue often chivvies, when I'm chopping up veg or preparing a salad. 'I'm hungry! Are you growing that lettuce from seed, or what?' Sue would have had the lunch made twice as fast, but I like to take my time, and for everything to be done perfectly. We have an ongoing joust about whether I'm a perfectionist (my opinion) or 'slightly anal', as Sue would have it. 'It'll be worth waiting for,' I say. 'Yes, but the trouble is, I might have passed out by the time it's ready,' she replies.

The Japanese way of life really impressed me. There was order and organisation, and I found that calming. Everybody is working who wants to, whatever their age, and I didn't see a single person who was homeless. People show one another consideration, pedestrians walk on one side of the pavement so it's all very orderly, and there are lots of staff on duty wherever you go, so things work efficiently and everybody gets good service. 'I could get used to this,' I thought, feeling very much at ease as I drank it all in. I could never live there, mind you. For one thing, I'd have to have my shoes shipped in, because none of their fabulous soft leather shoes are made to fit my size eights, which was very disappointing. For another, Japanese food is not my favourite – I'd rather have a Sunday roast than sushi any day of the week. But Japan reinforced what I already knew about myself, and how I like to live, and that's so important to know. Be aware of what makes you feel calm and what stresses you out, and don't feel pressured to live in a way that works for somebody else, whether it's over big life decisions, or how to chop the iceberg lettuce! We're all different, and life is better for everyone when we're all allowed to do things our way.

* * *

Ed taught me a big lesson about looking after number one. It happened when he got involved with helping me sort out my finances. 'Sweetheart,' he said one day, 'it's lovely that you like to help other people, but you have to look after yourself first.' As soon as I started to do well I wanted to treat Mum and help her out financially, and the same was true with other members of the family. It's what anybody would do, but the issue was that I did it at a time when I had not one but two big mortgages. Without Ed, I hadn't seen the wood for the trees financially, but he was right – if I looked after my own affairs first, I'd actually be in a far better position moneywise, and in the long run that would benefit everybody else. It's no accident cabin crew always tell you to put your own life mask on before you help others, and Ed helped me see that this is a lesson that applies to life in general. It's not selfish to put yourself first, in fact the opposite is true, because when you're in good shape, you can take better care of friends, family members and partners, in every way.

Having a duvet day is one of my favourite ways of taking care of me. God, I love a duvet day! We all need time to ourselves, and it's fine to do nothing, it really is. It's also perfectly okay not to see anybody when you need to sort your head out; good friends will understand that. Having a day off the grid helps us decompress, it recharges us and it sets us up for the next adventure. And when we do emerge from under the duvet, we're a better person for it. To me it's such a treat to go back to bed with a cup of tea and a packet of biscuits. My mother was right about nearly everything in life, but not this. She never let me stay in bed, even when I was at my lowest ebb after Henrik left. It was a generational thing – duvet days were absolutely frowned upon in her day – but I think it's such a shift for the better that we allow ourselves to have them now. I put Netflix on, or I read something I can immerse myself in. At the minute that's romantic fiction by Milly Johnson, a fellow Yorkshire woman, and I can lose myself for hours in her books, which is just the best.

I've never been a morning person, so when I need to get up I always set the alarm half an hour earlier, to give myself plenty of time to come round and get in the right frame of mind. Sometimes I just think about the day ahead and what I want to achieve, or I listen to something inspirational, like the self-development app Headway, which sums up ideas from really interesting books. It's not always for me – there was one about a 'no spend challenge' recently and I thought, 'No, love, sorry, that's not gonna work for me!' – but it's up to you to listen to what *you* feel you need at the time. If I'm in the mood I write in my diary about what I feel grateful for, but I don't put myself under pressure to do it every day. After Ed passed there were days when I just didn't feel anything, and I couldn't be bothered. I rarely have those days now, but if I do, that's fine, because we're all allowed to have an off day.

I'm very fortunate to have a beautiful garden and some land at the back of the house. When the weather's good I take myself outside and walk around, looking at the trees and flowers and all the shrubs Ed and I planted together. At the same time I like to listen to something on Audible, and I'm usually out there for ages, so it's a good way of getting my steps in too. Yep, 'three jobs Jane' is at it again, but they are three of the things that relax me the most, and rejuvenate me.

When the mood takes me, I like nothing better than to sit at the piano and lose myself in playing or writing some music. I've got a white concert grand piano and it's my absolute pride and joy. Preparing for the tour has been brilliant, because I've been playing more than I have for a long time, and it's reminded me how important the piano is to me. As a child it gave me an escape from the bullies, both physically and emotionally, and all through my life it's been a source of comfort and happiness. We all have different interests, but I think it's so important to have time in your day where you do something for you, something you really enjoy. If you think you don't have time for a hobby, or to take time out in a busy day, put down your phone more often, and get off social media if you're on it. It's so easy to waste hours scrolling online and I refuse to do it, because time is so valuable, and we never get it back. I'd much rather be doing something that makes me feel calmer, happier and more at peace with the world. As soon as I lift the piano lid I feel happiness bubbling all the way to my fingertips, and I think how lucky I am to be able to play.

Before bed I like nothing better than soaking in the bath with some relaxing music playing. I put on electric candles – they're less fuss than real ones – and I feel all the stresses of the day melting in the bubbles. I've looked after me, and that feels so good; I'm sure RuPaul would give me a big 'hell yeah!'

But tomorrow's another day, and I want to keep growing and learning and being the best version of myself I can be. That's why, when I get up in the morning, I'll be asking the same question all over again when I look in the mirror: 'What can I do for me today?'

FINDING YOUR PURPOSE

'We're all put on this earth to do something'

'I've found my purpose in life,' I declared on *Lorraine*, in April of this year. I was working hard preparing for my 2024 tour and Ranvir Singh, who was the guest host that day, probably thought I'd be going on about rehearsals and venues. But no – here I was, getting all philosophical on daytime telly! I couldn't help myself, because putting the tour together has been something else, it really has. Since losing Ed I've learned so much about myself, why I'm here and where I want to go next. And when I sat in that armchair, I just had to share what was in my heart.

When I was younger, watching Shirley Bassey and Cilla with starry eyes, I wanted to be like them. It was all about my hopes and dreams and what I wanted to do with my life. When I actually got on stage and put on a show, I was ecstatic, and I wanted to do it again and again. I loved seeing the audience have a good time, but most of all I was happy to be living out my dream. After that, all I wanted to do was keep improving my act, play better venues and see my name up in bigger and brighter lights. It's very different now. My focus has shifted, and I'm looking at the landscape of my life from another perspective.

We are all put on this earth to do *something*, and every one of us has a purpose. Some are great mothers or fathers, or amazing friends, role models or carers. My purpose in life is to entertain, and believe it or not, it's only recently that I've realised this. I am here to write and sing songs that people can relate to, and are touched by, and I'm here to get on that stage and give the audience a fabulous night. 'It's not your voice, it's ours,' my lovely fan Jeni memorably said, when I said I was retiring from touring after losing Ed. It had seemed like the right thing to do at the time. Finishing off that last tour nearly killed me, and there was a particular moment of clarity one morning, when Sue looked at me and said: 'What are we doing?' It was 5am and we were getting off the tour bus in a car park somewhere, still in the clothes we had on the night before because we'd been so wiped out when we finally got to our beds. 'I don't know,' I said. 'We really don't need to be doing this, do we? Not at our age!' As it turned out, announcing I was going to retire was the best thing I did, because that's what prompted Jeni to speak out. And that was the moment when I started to see things in a totally different light.

Nothing is about me anymore. The audience comes first, second and third, and that's the reason I'm touring again. I can't *not* do it; it feels like the fans and the universe have joined forces to pull me back to the stage. I'm so lucky, because I know when I'm out there I'll enjoy myself as much, if not more than, the fans, and I'll be so thrilled to be back.

I've called the tour *With All My Love* because I want to thank every person who comes to see me, and I want everyone in the audience to feel a huge amount of love from the stage, because they are the most important people in the room. I owe my fans everything, because without their encouragement and support, I wouldn't have made it back, not just this time, but so many times before.

If Ed were still here, I'd probably be happily mooching around, enjoying retired life with him. But when you lose someone, all the plans you had together are torn up and thrown in the air. When those pieces eventually begin to drift back down to earth you have a whole new set of decisions to make, about which direction to go in next. It's not easy. The grief never leaves you, and I have to make a decision every morning about what my day is going to be like. You can go one way or the other, but I always try to choose the positive way, telling myself that there is a bright side to everything in life, and life is for living. Ed's passing gave me the space to be able to respond to Jeni's powerful words in the only way I could. Finding your purpose in life is like a kind of enlightenment, or at least it has been for me. At last I can see very clearly what I'm here for, and what I need to go out and do, and I feel *wonderful*.

✳ ✳ ✳

It can take a very long time to work out what your purpose in life is, and that's okay. In my case, it's taken more than six decades, for heaven's sake! Looking back, I can see I've been working towards this moment my whole life long, and in so many different ways: I've learned from the wisdom of my family and friends, I've learned from all the opportunities, obstacles and challenges life has put before me and, more recently, of course I've learned from my fans, because they are the ones who opened my eyes to a whole new view of my world.

From my toddler years, when Gran decided I had 'something a wee bit special' and was preparing for my 'destiny' as I waved from the window to the people at the bus stop outside our house, it seemed like the die had been cast on my future. Gran and Mum both firmly believed I was going to do something 'different' and when I decided for myself that I wanted to make a career out of singing, Mum went a step further in sharing her opinion.

'I don't think you are on this earth to get married and have children,' she told me.

'Really?' I said.

'No, you've got dreams. You have other things to do.'

I think this conversation took place after I had failed as a dancer, and when I went back to work at Casanova's, when I was still in my teens. It was a surprising thing to hear at such a young age, but I wasn't shocked by it. By then I'd already laid the foundations of a career in entertainment, and having children one day had never entered my head. I had never been a girl who dreamed of a big white wedding, or imagined what names I would give to my children, and I couldn't imagine that ever changing. Even my cautious Dad told me he thought I would achieve my dream. 'I know you'll be brilliant at being a singer,' he told me. 'You're different, Jane, and you can be anything you want to be. Just have a back-up plan, and always put something by for a rainy day, that's all I'll say.' Such faith and encouragement from the people I looked up to the most in the world empowered me to keep going as I worked my socks off pursuing my career, and picking myself back up every time something went wrong.

When I was a small girl, incapable of even riding a bike without getting travel sick, Gran told me she saw a lot of wheels, cars, planes and trains in my future, and that I was going to travel all over the world. My grandmother had a very good reputation at the Spiritualist church, and by all accounts there was no doubting her psychic abilities. Her comments inevitably had an impact on me. As unlikely as it seemed, maybe I would turn out to be a globetrotter? If Gran foresaw it, there had to be some truth in it.

Mum didn't inherit Gran's psychic abilities – something she was furious about – but that didn't stop her being a regular up at the Spiritualist church. She never put pressure on any of us to follow suit, and Dad was a non-practising Catholic with no interest in attending any church. It meant the only formal religious education I got was at school, in general RE lessons.

'You have to find what talks to you,' Mum always said. 'Go and find your own religion.'

When Gran made her predictions, my mother always told me to pay attention, but to make my own mind up what to do with the information. 'Listen to your gut and then decide, and that will be the right thing to do.'

About three weeks after Dad passed, my mother told me she had a dream about him being on a farm. There were horses in the fields, including a big white stallion, and my dad was there with his father. I told Mum I thought it was a lovely dream, because it obviously meant father and son had been reunited when Dad passed over. I didn't think any more of it. A few weeks later, Mum suggested we go along to a psychic evening in Rotherham, which was being hosted by an old friend of mine, Steve Holbrook, who had become a very well-known psychic. 'Why not?' I said. Mum had passed on her open-mindedness to me, and it was always great to see Steve.

When me and Mum arrived at the venue it was packed out, and we didn't have tickets. 'Never mind, Mum,' I said, looking at the people queuing around the block. 'It obviously wasn't meant to be.' Just at that moment Steve appeared – he'd nipped outside for a fag break – and he insisted on squeezing us in somewhere.

A female clairvoyant was the first person to take to the stage. 'I want to speak to someone who's just lost their father,' she said. A few hands went up but I shrank back into my seat. The woman went on to say that this particular father had passed away very early in the morning, which gave me a start. Mum and I were sat up in the gods where I hoped I might be safe, but straight away the woman homed in on me.

'Is it you, with the red coat on?'

'Yes,' I said meekly.

'Well, your dad is here, and he's saying there's nowt wrong with your voice. There's a ship. You need to go and work on it, and let your mother grieve. You are being strong for each other but you both need to grieve. You need to do your life and she needs to do hers.'

As I sat there, feeling the hair standing on the back of my neck, the woman then spoke to my mother, telling her that Dad was saying he was sorry, but he was on the farm now, with the horses, and she didn't need to worry. Mum and I looked at each other in shock. 'Well, if we don't believe now we never will!' she said.

None of this came as any surprise to Gran, of course. When I got a job on a huge cruise ship called *Horizon*, in the early nineties, I can remember how I excitedly told my grandmother I was going to New York for rehearsals, because the shows I'd be taking part in were very glitzy and extravagant, and I had to learn the sets and be very polished and professional. This was a big deal for me and I was really excited, but Gran didn't turn a hair. 'I always knew you were destined for something special,' she nodded. 'Oh, is that it?' I thought. I'd been hoping for a bit more of a fanfare!

Another time I told Gran I was hoping my next contract would be with a cruise company called Silversea, because it would mean I could get to see parts of Asia and Australia.

It was 1995 and Gran was very elderly and frail by this time, but she told me sharply it was not my destiny and I needed to stay on the ship with the cross. My heart sank as I pictured the blue cross logo of Celebrity Cruises, the company I was currently with. I really didn't want to stay there as I felt there were much better prospects for me with Silversea, but when I explained this to Gran she shook her head and stuck doggedly to her prediction. Then she went further. Not only did I need to stay on the ship with the cross, I was going to meet a man called Henry. 'Really?' I said, eyes widening. This seemed very unlikely to me. It's a popular name now, but it wasn't then, at least not in my age group. I gave a little laugh and decided to take all of Gran's words with a pinch of salt.

I'd always listened to Mum's advice about making decisions based on your gut instinct, rather than living your life by psychic predictions. People went to the Spiritualist church for comfort and direction, she said, or confirmation and validation for a choice already made. 'If you don't agree with what the psychic tells you, you don't do it,' she would say. 'Ask yourself, what do *you* want to do?' I lost count of how many times she said that over the years. 'What's your gut saying, Jane? That'll give you the answer.'

Chapter Ten

When Silversea made me an offer I decided to go for it, despite what Gran had said. It would be a good move career-wise, and that's all I was interested in. Except things did not go the way I expected them to and, as it turned out, delays with the Silversea job meant I ended up taking another contract with Celebrity instead, joining a cruise ship called the *Century*. You heard me, the *Century* – the same ship on which I met Henrik! When we got together I was so caught up in my new romance that it took my mother to point out that Gran had been right, not just about me staying on the ship with the cross, but about meeting a man who was (almost) called Henry. What can I say? And if I hadn't stuck with Celebrity, I would never have become the headline act on their new ship the *Galaxy*, or found myself being filmed for *The Cruise* . . .

Some of the good friends I made at sea got to hear my stories about my psychic grandmother, and one day they bought me a pack of tarot cards and asked me to give them a reading. The rule is you cannot buy your own cards, and seeing as they'd gone to the trouble I thought I'd better give it a go. Before I started, I read everything I could about tarot, wanting to give it my best shot. I found it all very interesting, and I learned that tarot is all about what you feel when you shuffle the cards, and when the person in front of you shuffles the pack. Really, all you are doing is tuning into the other person and their vibrations, and so the cards are just a prop.

I did readings for loads of people over the next few weeks. I'm not sure what I expected, but some of the things I started to come out with spooked me. 'I think we'd better stop,' I said, because stuff I said, about who would end up with who, or which person would get the next job, were all starting to be a bit too accurate. 'No, you can't stop!' my friends said. They couldn't get enough of it, and so I kept it up for a bit longer. I might have only been in my thirties, but I was starting to feel like the wise old woman of the sea as I sat there, talking about life and love and everything in between! Eventually, I called it a day when I realised all I was doing was listening, talking and letting people make up their own minds, so what was the point in the cards?

'Just come and have a chat,' I ended up saying. 'We don't need these cards.' I do believe there is something out there and that the universe can speak to you, and you to it. What 'it' is, I have no idea, but I don't think that matters. I've read a lot about other religions in my time, and I've come to the conclusion the one thing we all have in common is faith, and some belief in there being something bigger than us. What works for me is being open-minded, and tuning into nature and how my interactions with the world make me feel.

My mother once told me that one of the hardest things in life is finding out what you're looking for, and what you want from it. 'Once you find it, it's very easy,' she said. 'You will know.' I'm not sure I fully understood what she was saying at the time, but I do now.

∗ ∗ ∗

When I was working as the headline act on the *Century*, if someone had told me that just a few years in the future I'd be putting on my own show at the MGM Grand in Las Vegas, I'd have thought I'd died and gone to heaven. That would be the dream come true, and I knew *exactly* how it would feel to see my name in lights in an iconic venue like that. Oh my God, it would be like all my Christmases had come at once. I'd give the performance of a lifetime and I'd feel on top of the flipping world!

Well, I got that wrong, didn't I? When I actually did perform at the MGM Grand, in 2002, the reality was devastatingly different. My career was already in reverse gear, with the BBC and my record label both stepping back from me. And I was also in Vegas when I first realised that my marriage to Henrik was on the rocks. We stayed in the most fabulous hotel suite, and we should have been having the time of our life, but it wasn't like that at all. During the trip we had just one night to ourselves, or so I thought. I hoped we could have an intimate dinner together, just the two of us, but as it turned out Henrik had invited some members of the press to join us. My career was sinking as fast at the *Titanic*, so I had to sit there trying to play the part of the successful singing star and happy wife. I felt so sick and scared, and I was feeling incredibly lonely in my marriage.

On the night of the show, the very last thing I felt like doing was putting on a sparkly frock and a big smile, but of course that's exactly what I had to do. From the outset I knew it would be a challenge connecting with an international audience in Vegas. I was used to chatting to Brits about *Emmerdale* or *Coronation Street*, and woe betide anyone if they went to the toilet in the middle of my show. 'Don't think I haven't noticed, I'm onto you!' I'd say. Henrik had told me repeatedly to stop the chatter, and believe me I tried. But I couldn't help it, and still can't. It's just a bit of nerves I think, and it's who I am.

'Don't blather,' I told myself before the curtain went up. 'Whatever you do, don't blather.' I did manage to button it more than usual, but I hadn't anticipated just how deep I'd have to dig to get through the show. When you're on stage it's up to you to create the energy and the atmosphere and make sure everyone is having a good time. If you're not in the best place in your personal life, that's a very tough gig, even when you're in the working men's club down the road, with all your mates there, rooting for you to do well. To pull it out of the bag in Vegas was one of the hardest things I've done, but I did it, and I got a good DVD to prove it, thank God. Every performer has to put on an act sometimes, but I deserved an Oscar that night, I really did. It was a truly horrible experience from top to bottom, and I couldn't wait to get out of the place.

On the flight out of Vegas I watched the dazzling lights on the Strip fading away from me as I reflected on the last few years, with Henrik at the helm of my ship. Fair's fair, he'd not only got me on stage in Vegas, he'd also got me my own BBC1 show on Saturday night TV. As I've said before, they were the two golden tickets I wanted, and he delivered both.

Star for a Night did well. It went from being a one-off special to running for a couple of years, and we discovered Alexandra Burke and Joss Stone when they were still kids. Hosting a primetime show was a massive feather in my cap, and it was the biggest entertainment show on BBC1 for a time. But was it the big prize I thought it would be? Honestly, the answer is no. I was under a huge amount of pressure, because I'd never done anything like it before and it was blooming hard work. I travelled all over the UK auditioning contestants, and in the studio it felt like mayhem all the time, constantly juggling between the acts, judges and special guests. I could handle that now, but back then I wasn't used to it – I mean, the chocolate buffet on the cruises was about the biggest distraction I was used to dealing with when I was in the spotlight!

I spent a lot of time wondering when I was going to be found out. And to cap it all, I was in that frustrating stage of my career when I'd been styled to oblivion and didn't recognise myself with my short hair and even shorter vowels. It was extremely stressful. I never felt I had the control I needed, so I was ill at ease and didn't feel I could give 100 per cent. Still, I have no regrets. It was always going to be difficult cutting my teeth as a TV presenter, but I'd done it, and I was incredibly lucky to have had the opportunity.

Star for a Night taught me a lot about myself and my career. Be careful what you wish for; that's the biggest lesson I took from that experience, and also from my performance in Vegas. Sometimes what you strive for is not the glittering prize you thought it would be, so think carefully before you hang your hat on goals and 'must-haves'. It's far better to think about what purpose you want your achievements to serve. If job title or kudos are the driving forces, think again, because those things alone won't bring you happiness, and so this isn't the right path for you. There is also no guarantee that if you climb up to a certain rung on the ladder, you are destined to keep going higher. So choose your steps carefully.

By the end of *Star for a Night* I was short-tempered with everyone and behaving like a pain in the backside, complaining about my hotel room when there was really nothing wrong with it, and similar such nonsense. That taught me another big lesson. When you are in a situation that isn't right for you, and you don't feel in control, you try to take control somehow and your stress has to come out somewhere. And that's when you start to behave in a way you really don't want to. That's what happened in my case, at least. And it's why nowadays I make sure I'm in control of everything in my life, and why I ask myself all the time, 'What purpose is this serving?' I also think very carefully about what I do next, and I make sure I'm surrounded by supportive people who aren't trying to change me. It's better for everyone, believe me!

* * *

My fans have played the biggest role of all in helping me find my purpose in life, and my relationship with them has evolved in a magical, marvellous way over the years. I can remember the first time I started to recognise faces in the crowd, so many years ago, and that gave me such a boost. 'Hello, love!' I'd say, catching someone's eye and giving a wave. 'How are ya?' I was always delighted to see familiar faces and it gave me a lot of confidence to know people were coming back to see me a second time, and then a third. I appreciated the support so much; it meant everything to me.

I was under no illusion I had my work cut out to keep up the momentum started by *The Cruise*. The TV viewers liked the fact I was a straight-talking northerner, happy to share my lows as well as my highs. But being a surprise hit on docusoap – just for being me – was one thing. Sustaining a new singing career off the ships, and on bigger and bigger stages, was quite another. What if fans of the TV show bought my new album just because of my name, and then were disappointed by it? Or what if they came to one concert and said 'never again'? That's why it was so incredibly uplifting to see the same people coming back for more. I had fans, and I can't tell you how much reassurance that gave me. I am *eternally* grateful to each and every one of them.

I loved going to the stage door after a show to meet the fans, sign autographs and thank them for being there. It was a fantastic part of the night, and in time I not only recognised faces, I started to get to know people and find out a bit about their lives. I also started to realise that there are fans, and then there are superfans. People formed friendships with each other on the back of following me around the country, and these lovely people started to meet up before concerts, go for dinner and even plan holidays together, organised around seeing one of my shows. Some have been friends for ten or twenty years now. It's very flattering that I'm the common denominator in their lives, but that's all I am. The rest is all them, their shared love of life and the fact they enjoy a great night out in good company. I'm in awe of them, I really am.

When I decided to tour again, I talked to Sue about the reasons why. 'I'm not getting any younger!' she grumbled. 'I thought you'd said enough was enough.'

She wasn't serious (although I did end up promising to bring in a new hair and make-up artist, so she could concentrate on being my PA). Things would be so much easier with Live Nation and Cuffe and Taylor on board too, and Sue fully understood my reasons behind my change of heart, and how I felt about the fans.

Sue is always the first one to point out special moments with the fans, like the times we've seen grown men cry buckets when I sing 'The Hand That Leads Me', or when we've watched elderly couples getting to their feet and dancing like demons to the disco medley. It's always so heart warming to see groups of girl pals sharing the love as they sing along together, and to meet the younger fans, in their twenties, who tell me they see me as their 'mad Auntie Jane' and just love spending the evening with me and the band. All of those things bring a tear to my eye, and give me a reason to go on.

Jolie Murrell and Katie Abbot are two incredible young women who have been following me for many years. Jolie used to watch me on *Loose Women* when she was 13 and on a break from home schooling. Can you believe it? When I started to get to know her, she told me that when I spoke about bullying one time it really resonated with her, making her feel less alone. I had no idea, and that was so touching to hear. Jolie came to her first concert when she was 14, and since then she and Katie have come to see me more than 100 times, including in Rhodes. Katie was 13 when I first met her at the stage door after a show. She and Jolie were very shy teenagers when they found each other at one of my concerts. At the time I had a much older audience and they wanted to bring younger people along, so they started 'TeamJMD', and now run fan pages on Instagram and X. They have become best friends, and it has been such a pleasure to see both girls blossom over the years. Today they live life to the full, are very popular with the fans and bring a sense of fun, putting videos on TikTok. How cool is that? Jolie has three tattoos in my honour, including some of the lyrics to the song 'The Rose'. She asked me to hand write them for the tattooist to copy, which I wasn't sure about at first. What if she regretted it? But she convinced me she was going to be a fan for life, so I let her persuade me. I always look out for both girls at the shows because their support means so much. Jolie and Katie have been phenomenal, they really have. They are there for me, and I'm there for them. That's what it's all about.

Another story that warms my heart involves Sue's son, Gareth. He used to be very quiet and not go out a lot, but a few years ago he met a lovely woman called Adele at one of my concerts. They became a couple and have enriched each other's lives immensely. They go everywhere together, enjoying shows and weekends away, and most of all they have someone to call their own. Their lives have changed so much because they went to my concert and found each other. It's beautiful, isn't it?

In 2019, when I found out that Radio 1's Adele Roberts took a framed photo of me as her luxury item when she went into the *I'm a Celebrity* camp, I nearly fell over. Her camp-mates were a bit nonplussed but, bless her, Adele told them I was the queen of Wakefield, and that the picture would remind her to 'go for life'. Apparently, listeners to her Radio 1 show would phone up and request a 'bit of Jane' if they were in a slump or feeling down, to help get them through the day. Oh my God, that's it, right there – all the validation I could ever wish for!

I have lots of truly amazing fans in the LGBTQ+ community too, and apparently I'm a 'hun', alongside fabulous women like Alison Hammond, Gemma Collins, Natalie Cassidy and Denise Welch. For the uninitiated (as I was, not too long ago), let me try to explain what I've learned about this lovely accolade. A hun is a woman who lives her best life, boldly. She's glam but gritty with it, she can be a bit camp and cheeky with her humour – intentionally or otherwise – and she has a down-to-earth attitude to food, holidays, having a laugh with friends and appreciating a good cup of tea, or perhaps 'some wines', like Pamela in *Gavin & Stacey*. A hun might be a bit of a diva – surely that can't be right?! – and she may be considered a national treasure. Or she can be both. Either way, she is 'iconic', but probably only in a low-key way. Whatever! I'll take low-key iconic, and if people say I'm a hun, who am I to argue? It's a great honour to be in the club.

Sue likes to know what people are saying and she's braver than me at reading comments online. 'This is a good one, you've got to hear this,' she says from time to time. 'Go on,' I say, bracing myself. God knows what she keeps from me – I'm sure there are some corkers she's kept to herself – but I'm grateful to her for sharing the nice ones, because they are a lovely reminder of why I do what I do.

'I've been on my hols with Jane tonight!' someone said recently, in response to my holiday show on the Canaries. That made my day. Whether I'm on telly or on stage, I want to make people smile and to make them feel a bit better, because finding joy is so important, to all of us. I got so much pleasure recently from watching the comedy-drama *Ted Lasso*. When I was told it was about a football coach I really wasn't sure it was for me, which is why it took me so long to get round to watching. But honest to God, I have never had so much enjoyment from a TV show. The performances are superb – Hannah Waddingham is my hun, let me tell you – and it touched me and entertained me like nothing I've seen before. 'Wow,' I thought. 'What a gift to create something like this.' That's the power of great entertainment, and if I can deliver a fraction of that enjoyment to people who come to see me, I'm winning.

* * *

I played at the Watford Colosseum in 2016, and after the show the theatre received a menacing phone call from someone who said he was waiting outside for me. I was told to stay in the dressing room while Martin went outside and explained to all the fans at the stage door that that they should go home, for their own safety. Sue and I had driven ourselves to the theatre that night, and when the police arrived they insisted on giving us a police escort home. If I'm honest, I thought it was all a bit over the top. Maybe this person just had a bad day? But no, the police officers were taking it very seriously indeed. They told me I was putting myself in a very vulnerable position, and that the stage doors needed to stop, completely. I couldn't believe it. I'd been meeting fans after the show for years, spending hours chatting, giving them a hug and posing for a photo.

'I don't really have to stop this, do I?' I said to Sue when the officers had left us. 'Honestly, it's too important. It's a massive part of the evening.' One look at Sue and I knew what she was going to say. She had been worrying about my security for a while, especially as the crowds were getting bigger and bigger.

'Jane,' she said bluntly, 'when the police tell you not to do something, you don't do it.'

I knew in my heart she was right, but it was a big blow, and I had to find a way around it. We tried meet and greets but they were no good for me, because you're meant to have a brief chat and photo and quickly move on to the next person in line. I was hopeless, gabbing to everyone for ages, and then discovering I'd spent longer on the meet and greets than I did on stage, there was still a massive queue and everything had run into overtime! The fan holiday to Rhodes was a much better idea. Though the timing wasn't brilliant for me, with Ed's passing being so recent, it was a huge success and the fans loved it. My plan now is to do a similar trip, but this time on a cruise. I've been wanting to do this since before lockdown, but life had other ideas. Now it feels like something that can't *not* happen, and it makes me go a bit giddy just thinking about it. Imagine it: my love of singing and cruising colliding, with my fans all around me, having a blast on the open seas. Forget Vegas – this is my idea of living the dream, and I want to do it for them as much as for myself.

I will never forget that it's the fans who have carried me through all the storms in my career, and I love them to bits, I really do. In the past I used to look out at a packed theatre and feel amazed that so many people knew the words to my songs, or got to their feet to applaud. I didn't quite believe they were all here for me, enjoying being entertained by me. 'I don't deserve this,' I thought. 'This can't be right.' I've learned that to believe in yourself, you have to know who you are, and what you stand for. When strangers in the industry tried to manufacture me into a polished 'product' I wasn't free enough or strong enough to tell them to leave me be, and let me do it my way. Thank God that's all ancient history now. Thanks to everything I've learned in life, going right back to my childhood, I know who I am, and I believe in myself and what I'm doing. And that's how you find out what your purpose is.

My mother was right when she said motherhood was not for me. Men are very secondary in my life and always have been, and writing this book has reminded me of lots of reasons why! I'm not looking for love, but if it comes my way, who knows? You can never say never. Mum never had another man after Dad passed away, but she'd spent her married life at odds with Dad over so many things, and I think it was a relief to her to have the freedom to finally get to do whatever she wanted without having a fight about it. 'Always be independent,' my mother told me repeatedly when I was a young woman. 'Have your own money. Never depend on a man.' Though she would never have told me what to do, she always stuck to her guns about the fact she didn't think I was meant to have children. I never had the yearning to be a mother. The maternal instinct was just not there, and I made a choice very early on that I was going to give 100 per cent to my career. I have no regrets. None whatsoever. Some people are born to be mothers and some are not. My mum's purpose was to be a mother and she was fantastic at it, but it was never my purpose, and I've always been fine with that.

I spent a lot of time in my late twenties and early thirties being single, and relatives, neighbours and even people I barely knew would ask me about boyfriends and future plans. Honest to God, I was like Bridget Jones, trying to avoid the awkward questions at the Christmas buffet, and cringing when people put me on the spot. When I married Henrik, I got another barrage of questions, this time from journalists too. Did we want to start a family? The clock was ticking, wasn't it time we got started? At the time I didn't feel I could say: 'No, the motherhood gene is missing!' and I skirted around the subject, but I wish I hadn't. Nobody should have to apologise or make excuses for choosing not to have children. It's perfectly okay not to want to be a parent, and if that is not your purpose, don't feel you have to explain yourself to anyone. The same goes for *everything* in life: it's up to you to discover what your purpose is, and it's up to everybody else to accept you for who you are, and the path you choose to tread.

The older I've become, the more I've grown into myself as a performer. I want people to come to my shows and go, 'Bloody hell, I wasn't expecting that!' Taking the piano and playing my own songs on tour is something I wouldn't have had the balls to do without the backing of my fans. That's another thing I will never be able to thank them enough for. They've been the ones who've encouraged me to take risks, and it's all thanks to them that I've been able to come back when I've been rejected, had my heart broken, lost everything I worked so hard for and had so many doors slammed in my face. The fans have stuck around, and without them I would be nowhere.

Mum was right about another thing: once you've found your purpose in life, everything just comes together. That's how it feels right now. My music, getting back with my band and writing new songs; that is what has given me such joy and a purpose since losing Ed. And as soon as I started working on this tour, it gave me a new lease of life. I came on in leaps and bounds and I felt myself growing every day, and wanting to do more. Good God, I've even agreed to play Maid Marion to Julian Clary's Robin Hood in panto at the London Palladium this year. Yes, I know I vowed I would never do another one, but how could I resist working with Julian? The man is panto royalty, and I've fallen in love with him already. Besides, I'm not looking behind me (sorry, couldn't resist that either!). I'm looking forward every day. All I had to do was think about how much fun everybody was going to have in that theatre – and at Christmastime too – and the answer had to be yes.

Whatever your purpose in life, whoever you are, and whatever you have been through, we all have it in us to create a joyful, happy life for ourselves. So go on – let the light in, make a difference, and be who you want to be. It's not always easy, but I can promise you, it's worth it.

EPILOGUE

When I compared my journey through life to flying the trapeze, in a hurricane, on board a ship, I wasn't wrong. Writing my book has confirmed it, and how lucky am I?

Life is for living and I've certainly done that. And I intend to keep going, no matter which hurdles I have to jump next, how high the bar is raised or how difficult it is to cling on when the going gets tough. And it *will* get tough again, because that's the reality of life.

When I was younger I worried so much, about so many things. I can see myself sitting on the floor of a hotel room with my head in my hands. 'Why is this not working?' I'm asking myself. 'What am I doing wrong?' I wish I could tell my younger self to stop worrying. 'In a hundred years, you won't be here,' I'd say, 'and nor will anyone you know. Everything you worked so hard for will be gone, or belong to someone else. So keep following your dreams, and if you mess things up, have another go. If people don't like what you do, sod them! You have one life, so let yourself live it, without fear, because that will only hold you back. Keep learning from your mistakes, and you will succeed.'

* * *

When I was growing up I used to love listening to Gran and her friends talking. They were so wise, and over the years I've also learned so much from everyone I have ever spent time with, in relationships, at work, and including all my family, friends and so many fans. I'm grateful to everyone who's come in and out of my life and taught me something, and if sharing what I've learned helps someone else, in any way at all, I'll be so chuffed. I think we all have a duty to share the wisdom we collect in our lives. What others do with it is up to them, but at least we have opened our hearts and given generously.

My favourite saying of all is 'make space for great things to happen'. I often do a 'death clean' in my house, and if you've ever had to clear someone else's belongings after a bereavement, you'll know what I'm talking about. I chuck out all the stuff I no longer use, need or want, and it's a liberating process. I have that same approach to life in general. Why do we hold on to so much? Physically and mentally, it's good to let things go. For me, that's the most important lesson of all.

Epilogue

I'm a great aunt now, can you believe it? My brother's daughter, Katie, had a baby boy in October 2022, and then she took my breath away by asking me if it was okay if she called him Ed. I was so touched; what a beautiful thing to do. Little Ed is *adorable*, and this bundle of hope and happiness has brought so many blessings to us as a family. It's our job to guide him as much as we can, and I'm very happy indeed that Great Aunt Jane has plenty of experience to pass on!

I'm still learning myself, of course, and I'm never going to stop. Age is but a number and you are never too old to do anything. We think we've got lots of time, but we haven't. I know Ed would be so pleased I'm going back on tour. He would want me to strive for happiness and try to live my best life every day, and that's what I'm doing. It's what we should all do, no matter what happened yesterday and what might happen tomorrow. Don't look back. Chase joy, go for life and let yourself shine as brightly as you can.

ACKNOWLEDGEMENTS

The hardest question you're ever asked is 'what do you really want?' and if you ask anyone what they really want they will struggle to tell you. When you find the answer to that question then you're halfway there. I am eternally grateful to the people in my life who, one way or another, have helped me find my way to the happy place I am in today.

My thanks go to:

My mother, Jean, for her unconditional love, guidance and wisdom.

My father, Peter, for his strength, belief and help to get me started on my path.

My darling Ed, for showing me what a partnership is and teaching me so many valuable lessons, including how to rest. I was very blessed to have such a wonderful, lovely man in my life. I continue to be grateful every day for the 13 years we had.

My best friend, Susan Ravey. For her loyalty, honesty, laughter and being my guardian angel.

Everyone mentioned in this book, good or not so good, has been invaluable in my development and progress and I'm grateful to have met and learned from each and every one of them.

Huge thanks to my agents, KT Forster and Craig Latto, for making this book happen, and to the team at Ebury Spotlight, especially Lorna Russell, Michelle Warner, Patsy O'Neill and Natalia Goncalves, and the PR team at Midas, Hannah McDonald and Phoebe Williams.

Rachel Murphy, thank you for your time listening to me drone on and on and on . . .

But most of all for capturing me *exactly*. It's an emotional and frightening time writing about your past, but you were the perfect companion.